Life and Times of a Valley Boy in Wales

Gareth Lyn Jones

Published by Garn Press, LLC
New York, NY
www.garnpress.com

Copyright © 2023 by Gareth Lyn Jones

Garn Press and the Chapwoman logo are registered trademarks of Garn Press, LLC

All rights reserved. No part of this publication may be reproduced, distributed, or transmitted in any form or by any means, including photocopying, recording, or other electronic or mechanical methods, without the prior written permission of the publisher, except in the case of brief quotations for reviews and other noncommercial uses permitted by copyright law. For permission requests, please contact Garn Press.

Book and cover design by Denny Taylor, Garn Press
Cover Image by Gareth Lyn Jones

First Edition, November 2023

Library of Congress Control Number: 2023948777

Publisher's Cataloging-in-Publication Data

Name: Jones, Gareth Lyn.
Title: Life and Times of a Valley Boy in Wales / Gareth Lyn Jones.
Description: First edition. | New York: Garn Press, 2023.
Identifiers: LCCN 2023948777 | ISBN 978-1-942146-84-1 (pbk.)
Subjects: LCSH: Autobiography. | Families. | Families—History. | Working class families, Welsh. | Authors, Welsh. | Family vacations. | BISAC: BIOGRAPHY & AUTOBIOGRAPHY / Personal Memoirs. | FAMILY & RELATIONSHIPS / General. | FAMILY & RELATIONSHIPS / Family History & Genealogy | FAMILY & RELATIONSHIPS / Marriage & Long-Term Relationships. | FAMILY & RELATIONSHIPS / Parenting / General
Classification: LCC HQ503-1064 2023 (print) | DDC 640

LC record available at https://lccn.loc.gov/ 2023948777

For Sandra

Without whose help and encouragement,

This would not have been possible.

Acknowledgments

Twelve months ago, when I first had the mad cap idea about writing my life story, I thought to myself 'who on Earth would want to read it?' But my family gave me some encouragement by saying it would be nice for all the family to read about what my life was like. With the pandemic out of control, I thought it would keep my mind busy during such difficult times. The family also got together to complete the foreword to this book. Thank you for your devotion to us as your Grandparents, we are unbelievably proud of you all and for your continued support and encouragement.

Although I have a good memory, I have a big problem in the fact that I write like I think and being dyslexic means being unable to spell which is a massive disadvantage when it comes to writing. When I finished the story editing was going to be a problem. However, my good friend Matthew Cleverly came to my rescue and his son, who was an actor and playwright, had offered to edit my book for me. Matthew and I have been friends since childhood, and I am grateful for his lifelong friendship and encouragement to write my memoir. Without his great help and guidance, the book would never have taken off. To Matthew and his son, my sincere gratitude.

Furthermore, I have come to understand how difficult it can be to have your written work accepted by a publishing company let alone getting to the stage where it is published. However, Sandra mentioned what I was about to do to her cousin, Denny Taylor, who lives in New York, and Denny said she would have the book printed and submitted to the National Museum of Wales. This gave me the momentum to get going and complete the task at hand.

The one woman who I have the deepest gratitude for is my wife, Sandra. Thank you for the decades of unconditional love, support, and patience. I cannot express in words the pivotal role that you play in this family.

My final thank you is to you for making it to the end. I hope you've had good reading. A big thank you to my entire family for encouraging me to write.

Gareth L. Jones
October 2023

Foreword

by

Sinead Robinson John

My Granddaughter

When I was asked to reflect on the legend I get to call "Bamp" many words to describe him sprang to mind, but what significantly stood out when thinking about my Grandad is that I caught myself smiling. Many people find relationships between parents and their children differ significantly to the relationships forged between grandparents and their grandchildren, so when I was approached to write the foreword to this book, it was important that I captured my Bamp's personality through the eyes of all his offspring.

In Welsh Valleys since the 1950s to the present day the roles of men and women have evolved a great deal. Men were generally the 'bread winners', grafting for endless hours, whilst their wives stayed at home raising the children. Men rewarded themselves with a few beverages in their local pubs at the end of a hard day's work. Although these are the memories of Gareth's three girls, Lynne, Ceri and Helen, it is clear through conversations that their Dad managed to still find a balance between work, socialising and home life. My Mam says Bamp created little routines with the girls, which have shaped wonderful childhood memories that they reminisce on today.

One memory that was shared was bath time at the Jones household. When the three girls were young their dad would wash their faces, necks and behind their ears and then carry them into the living room where their Mam would dry and dress them ready for bed. He did this one by one. Although, he was out most nights when the girls were young, he always made sure he kept up special routines, including when he would come upstairs and say, "goodnight big rabbit," "goodnight medium rabbit," and "goodnight baby rabbit."

Being a steadfast figure in all our lives, Bamp's paternal role in his children's and grandchildren's lives will stay with us forever as he continues to inspire, guide and nurture us all into and through our adult lives. Those who know Gareth Jones, know his inability to filter his words. Although at times it has been said that this trait can be 'infuriating', it is also a part of his personality that is loved and respected. His honest opinions and advice have allowed us to turn to him for support and advice and share in his wisdom. His ability to speak the truth has also shaped our personalities in ways that we can reflect on ourselves, speak the truth, take the truth or simply disagree with the opinions of others.

The different ages of his grandchildren have meant that Bamp has had a different role in each of their lives. My early memories of my Bamp are of him reading to us. I remember he would read to me, and I would read to him. Our whole family still revels in his ability to tell us stories. He has an amazing memory, and his vivid and colourful imagination made the tales he tells even more mesmerising. Friends of Bamp's will know this is true, enjoying his stories as much as we do.

Bamp's ability to work with his hands has been passed on to his grandchildren. We all helped him in the garden where he grew vegetables and flowers, and shed where he did his woodworking. These experiences inspired his two eldest grandsons Daniel and Conor to become carpenters. With Bamp's extremely high standards with carpentry, it was inevitable that his grandsons would adopt these standards and become so successful in their trade.

Reflecting upon my grandparents, it is fascinating to realise the interconnections between us all. Their morals, values and personality traits are woven into our DNA by Nan and Bamp, the creators of our family. Each of us, his children, grandchildren, and great grandchildren, possess a trait of Bamp's. His daughter Ceri and her daughter Cerys share his need to have a clean and organised home, his eldest daughter Lynne and her daughter Chloe share his outspoken, honest and fearless attitude, his grandsons Conor and Euan share his passion to entertain and his love to emerge in a good sing song, Daniel and Thomas share his love for sport, and his youngest daughter Helen and I have gained his creative genes. But it's Bamp's unwavering work ethic and loyalty that has undoubtedly been passed down to each and every one of his children and grandchildren. He is honourable, decent, and kind.

Daniel shared a memory of when he was ten years old after playing well in a school rugby match watched by Bamp. He came into the room where Daniel was resting his aching muscles and said with a proud look on his face "you was outstanding today pal". Daniel stated that, "It was from that moment that I believed I must have something special and that he would always be my biggest fan".

You see, some people find it easy to tell their loved ones how much they are loved. Saying "I love you" is not Bamp's way of showing his love and pride. Instead of hearing it, we feel it. We feel it in all the stern conversations he's had with us about making better choices and being the best versions of ourselves. We feel it when he's stood on the side-lines of all the rugby and football matches, he's attended. We feel it through his unwavering presence through all the ups and downs we've experienced as a family, and we feel it when his face lights up and his energy shoots through the roof when his great grandchildren enter the room. As the author and activist, Maya Angelou wrote, "People will forget what you said, people will forget what you did, but people will never forget how you made them feel".

Behind every great man is an even greater woman. The patience, commitment, and unconditional love of our Nan, Sandra have complimented his personality and allowed my Bamp to be the person he is today. Their long-term marriage has shown us what real love looks like. The unbreakable bond they share resonates within us all and allows us to grow together as a family. As the matriarch to our family, she is unaware of how her gentle but fiercely protective nature has also positively shaped all our lives. It is their partnership that has equipped us all with the morals and values we all possess today and hopefully will pass down to future generations.

The fact that Bamp has written this book at a fearful time in history shows the relentless and resilient nature of Gareth Jones. Since the date this book was written, Bamp, who is nearly 80 years of age at the time that I write, has enrolled in a number of learning courses, again showing that learning is a lifelong endeavour. He has also welcomed two more beautiful Great-Granddaughters into our ever-growing family; Fleur May Jones and Lyla-Rose Worwood and another Granddaughter on the way.

As a family we hope that you enjoy the emotional roller coaster on which you are about to embark on, and that you revel in Bamp's nostalgic memories of what it was like living in the Welsh Valleys.

Sinead Robinson-John
October 2023

Introduction

The Ninth of November 2020

I started writing this book at 8:25 on the 9th of November 2020. This year has been one of the most devastating years in the history of the British Isles. Since March, we have been in the grip of a pandemic which has taken over us, and the rest of the world. In January, our country was alerted to a virus that started in China. At the time we thought nothing of it, but very quickly new words have appeared in our daily lives, such as: pandemic, COVID-19, lockdown, self-isolate, and coronavirus. My wife, Sandra and I have been what the government called "shielding," because we have health problems and are getting on in years. Not being able to closely see our large family for some time has been very difficult for us. To pass the time I decided to put my life story down for future reading, and the words that you're currently reading are the result. It might be quite boring to some people, but hopefully interesting to a few, and hopefully, by the time you're reading this, things will be back to normal.

When I decided to write a book on my life – the life of a valley boy, I had a large problem. Although I have a good memory, I write like I think. Being dyslexic and not being able to spell is a great disadvantage. Anyway, I have gotten through. The person I owe this to is Sandra, my wife. Without her help and encouragement this would not have been possible. To have met and married someone like her after a particularly wild and boisterous life in Ebbw Vale beforehand is something I cherish daily. When we started our family on our wedding night, I never in my wildest dreams imagined I would end up with such a wonderful family. I have got three wonderful daughters, three wonderful granddaughters, four wonderful grandsons – two of which have followed me as carpenters, and the icing on the cake, which not many people live to see, the five best great-grandchildren anyone could hope for.

Part One

Being a Rhyd-y-Cae Boy

I was born on the 1st of May 1943 in 19 Carmeltown, Beaufort. Beaufort is a small hamlet near Ebbw Vale in the South Wales Valleys. The area is situated at the head of the South Wales Valleys, and the town, like many in South Wales, was born from the need for coal and limestone to make iron. The first iron works was started in 1779 in Beaufort and from there continued to spread across South Wales. The village of Beaufort is situated on the main trunk road between Merthyr Tydfil and Abergavenny, also known as the A465.

I was the second son to my parents Thomas Charles Jones and Mary Evelyn Jones née Jenkins. My father worked in the coal mines and was considered an essential worker. He served in the local Home Guard, and I was told that I was the result of when he came home from a week away at camp. Our cottage was the same as everyone else's in the area at that time: stone floors, and a tap for water; and a toilet at the bottom of the garden. Before this cottage, my parents had lived in rooms with other families, due to evacuation in WWII, so this cottage was considered a step in the right direction.

In 1944 my brother Graham, who is 11 years older than me, passed the 11 plus exam for entrance to the local grammar school; a fine achievement in those days. In 1946, my parents had the chance to move to a better house which was situated in the Rassau, not very far from Carmeltown. I was three years old and don't remember much of the move, but it was done in our local coal lorry, and I'm told it rained all day. The move was to 36

Rhyd-y-Cae, a fairly new house with three bedrooms and an inside bathroom. We were supposed to exchange houses with the family who lived at number 36, but on the day of the move the other family changed their minds and didn't want to swap. After a lot of argy-bargy, both sides agreed to share the house together. The other family were living in 36 because they had been evacuated because of the war. Now the war had ended, they were waiting to return to their home in Kent. They turned out to be a lovely family to live with, only staying one year. They were Mr and Mrs Bathurst and their son John. They all spoiled me rotten! I was heartbroken to see them leave. I remember in 1947 we had very heavy snow and their son John, who was a carpenter, made me a sledge out of an old table. Looking back, that small spark of joy may have been the reason I became a carpenter later in life!

36 Rhyd-y-Cae was a wonderful place to live. The houses in Rhyd-y-Cae were built in the shape of the horseshoe stood up on its points. We lived in the middle of the bend at the top of the hill. At the end of our garden, about 16 metres from the house was the main Abergavenny to Merthyr railway line, on which around 12 to 15 trains passed daily; a frightening prospect for some people, but one gets used to it.

Our neighbours were unbelievable! Mrs Aplin was my mother's best friend. She had a large family of boys: John, Harry, Morris, Peter, David, and her only daughter, Margaret was my first girlfriend. I was a very sickly child and the first call my mother made was always to Bridgy Aplin. When I was seriously ill with pneumonia Mrs Aplin saved the day. I wouldn't take antibiotics, so she managed to acquire a puppy to bribe me to take them. She would also frequently feed me because I would eat better at her house with her children. The other family I could be found hiding with were the Lisle's. My best friend, David Lisle (known as Dinkey to everyone), was the only boy in a family of seven girls. Mrs Lisle was a very small, religious, and nervous lady, but "the father" as everyone called him was a great block of a man who ruled with a loud, booming voice.

I started in Rassau School in 1948. I remember excitedly walking in because all the friends I had played with were with me. I don't remember much about the teacher, Mrs Roberts other than she was a very kind lady. I took to her immediately as she was the kind of person who made us all feel comfortable on that first day of school. I remember there was a giant sandbox for us to play in, and after lunch we would sleep on our desks and see if the fairies had come and cleaned the chalk off the board while we slept.

Rassau School was situated at the bottom of Rhyd-y-Cae on School Road. It was an old school. My mother and all her family had gone there, and at that time most of our family lived in the surrounding area of it. I had a lot of uncles, aunts, and cousins to bother with. I was very close to my cousin, David Jenkins, but when he passed his 11 plus exam to go to the grammar school, we went our separate ways. From an early age, I was a very outgoing person, making friends with lots of different children. My mother could never find me because in the 50s it was safe for children to play anywhere and everywhere outside, and I did. Quite often you would find her asking her neighbours "Have you seen our Gareth?" or just shouting "GARRRETH!" quickly followed by me emerging from someone else's house.

Our house was on the side of Rhyd-y-Cae with even numbers, and opposite were odd. Looking from our front door to the left took you down to the school and School Road. To the right led to the main Rassau Road, but there were only half as many houses on our side of the street. This was because of how the Cwm Nantmelyn Brook curves next to the Rhyd-y-Cae road going down the hill on our side of the street before joining the Rasa Brook. One of my mother's main concerns with me was that I was always playing in the river, which affected my health because I suffered with chest problems and tonsillitis.

Being a Rhyd-y-Cae boy at that time entitled you to become a member of the Rassau Army who joined the Graig-Ebbw and the Wain-Fawr boys when we went to war with the Carmeltown Gang. Ash bin lids wooden sticks and anything else were all fair game in our war. When November came around, it was all hands on deck to collect tyres, cut trees down for the street bonfire, but you'd have to watch out for other streets who might try to set it alight before Guy Fawkes Night.

Sport has been a huge part of my life, especially as I was growing up. My father was a goalkeeper for Ebbw Vale in his younger days and was a very good cricketer too. I remember riding the machines with him as a small boy when he would cut the cricket pitch. He also captained the collieries' cricket team. I watched but couldn't understand why they went into a pub after the game. We also played cricket in our back garden with my brother and our neighbour, Allun. Football also played a big part in my upbringing as I would kick a ball at our wall at the back of the house and imagine the two drainpipes were goal posts. I would imagine I was one of the Welsh players at that time notably, John Charles, Trevor Ford, and Ebbw Vale local boy, Ron Burgess.

One Christmas I was given a Cardiff City football kit and ball. I immediately became Alf Sherwood, captain of Wales. Not really a physically strong boy, I failed to get into the Rassau School soccer team. I think I might have excelled at cricket, but we only played it once in a while. Aside from sport, the street games we played were marbles or as some called them, arlies, Hide & Seek, Strong Horses & Weak Donkeys, Bat's Catty, and Hopscotch (when we could get chalk). A means of acquiring chalk was to go to the houses they were building over the river and get plasterboard to break up. A task only for the brave because the watchman was always on the lookout for us boys. We tormented this man and called him Billy Butter Balls. It was always quite cold up the Rassau in winter. When a hard Frost was about, we poured water on the concrete road to make a slide as there were barely any cars in those days. Knockout ginger was another game we'd play. We'd tie a string of cotton to someone's letterplate, and hiding behind the opposite wall, we'd pull it slightly to get them to come to the door. If you got caught, you got a clip across the ear or a kick up the arse. It was no good telling your parents or you would get another one.

Sunday in my house was a no play day. I had the weekly scrub on a Sunday morning ready to go to Sunday School in the afternoon and chapel in the evening. My mother was not a very religious person but being brought up in a religious household with my grandfather, who was a deacon in Caramel Congregational Chapel, gave her a sense of religious duty. After I'd return from Sunday school the order was to change from my best clothes into my old clothes; a task I carry out to this day. The best things about going to chapel were the yearly trips to Barry Island, Christmas parties, and games where you could kiss the girls. The downsides were the anniversaries when you had to learn a recitation and stand before the Sunday school in the afternoon and again in the night and say it to a full chapel - it filled me with terror!

One particularly memorable incident occurred the day I went missing. I was eight or nine years old at the time. All the normal houses I frequented were explored but I could not be found. Three hours had passed, and the police were about to be called when to everyone's amazement I strolled up the road without a care in the world. When quizzed about my whereabouts I told everyone I'd been in Melvin Lloyd's house, some distance away, and a place I had never been in my life before!

In 1950, when I was seven, my brother Graham, was called up to do national service in the army. He did his basic training in Devizes, Somerset. When he came home, I was proud to think that my brother was a real soldier in his uniform. As he was quite clever, he avoided an infantry regiment for the Royal Army Day Corps with a posting in Taunton Somerset. When he went away it gave me more freedom to explore further away from my house. One of my and my friend's favourite things to do was to put pennies and nails on the railway line for passing trains to flatten them. Some short distance from my house behind the back of my garden, was a small field where we all played: lighting fires, roasting potatoes, and damming the river to make paddling ponds. Across the river in the building site where we sometimes stole chalk was a place where we could also steal sand. We would take buckets of the stuff and bring it back to our den.

As my father worked in the Marine Colliery Cwm as a collier, we had plenty of coal. At that time, colliers had a ton of coal every month. Coal was precious and was used as a currency to barter for other things that were in short supply. After my father worked all day digging coal the last thing he wanted to do when he came home was put a ton of coal in the back garden. So, someone was always on the lookout to do the job for him. Big families always had butter or sugar to give away for a bucket or two of coal. My mother, like a lot of her brothers kept chickens and ducks. We also had our own eggs. She would hatch the chicks and keep cockerels for Christmas. Uncle Peter would come to kill them and then he would hang them up by their legs to die. I was always fascinated by this operation. My mother would then de-feather them and cut out their innards, which she threw on the fire to burn with the feathers – what a smell!

Selling the cockerels would help pay for Christmas. My mother would also make a special cake; about 8 loaves. It was the most beautiful cake anyone ever tasted. It took ages to make as the dough had to stand by the fire for hours for it to rise. Christmas morning was always a special occasion. My presents and our stockings full of nuts and fruit were always on the table which was pulled out. In those days, the dinner would be cooked on an old black fire grate, and the fire would rise halfway up the chimney. I remember on Christmas nights going down to Aunty Carries' which was my mother's childhood home. We'd go there for supper, dancing, and songs around the piano. When my father played cricket for Beaufort, he kept his cricket bag at home. So, as boys, we would get in the bag or attempt to use it to play in our back garden. When he went to play rugby matches away, he would look for a present to give us when he returned home; a thing I did in later years myself.

A highlight in our street was when Mr Aplin got a television. All the neighbours would queue outside to have a glance at the wonder of TV. His house was packed with people to watch King George's funeral, February 1952. The screen was only 10 inches by 10 inches, so he purchased a magnifying glass to go in front of the TV. It worked well if you were sitting or standing directly in front of the set, but you couldn't see a thing from the side! My brother Graham was demobbed from the army in November 1952, and with the money he saved he got us a television too. I remember coming home from school and seeing the double X aerial on the chimney. Joe Owen installed it - a fly type of bloke. After he installed things, you could never get him to come back to maintain them - as the well-known rhyme said about him:

> W J Owen TVision and sound,
>
> Whenever he's wanted, he can never be found.
>
> He had a shop in Carmeltown.
>
> Now the council have knocked it down.

The radio programmes I used to listen to including Dick Barton – Special Agent and Raiders in the Sky were all gone. We had the Queen's Coronation on television, June 2nd, and the sales of TV sets went through the roof. The best programmes of the time were The Flower Pot Men, Andy Pandy, and Watch with Mother.

School hadn't changed much for me since the day I started in 1948. Five years on and I could read, write, and count, but couldn't spell, and still can't after all these years! I've been on this earth 78 years, and it's too late now! Still, I was very good at playing and sport – pity those weren't included in the 11 plus exam – would've passed every time!

In the spring of 1953, my mother and Mrs Aplin decided to go to Newport to do some shopping. Normally they'd go by bus; a journey that took about just over an hour, but this time it was decided they'd go by train – even though neither woman was accustomed to train travel. So, it was down to Ebbw Vale station; my mother, me, Mrs Aplin, and Margaret (my first ever girlfriend). We got to Newport alright and enjoyed the day out. It got to late afternoon, and it was time to head back home. Newport, even in those days was a very busy place, and after much confusion we boarded a train that we thought was heading to Ebbw Vale. After a few miles, I remember thinking I don't think this is the right way. I didn't remember seeing certain landmarks that we were passing on the way down. I was politely told I had been looking through the other window, but after about an hour and still insisting that we were going the wrong way we stopped at a station and didn't start moving again. After 10 minutes, a guard opened the door and said: "What are you doing here? This train doesn't go any further. We're in New Tredegar. You're on the wrong train and you'll have to wait another hour to go back to Newport to catch the right train back to Ebbw Vale." When back in Newport we were still confused and had to be escorted to the Ebbw Vale train. That was the last time my mother and Mrs Aplin ever mentioned using the railway.

Later that year, after several bouts of tonsillitis I was taken to Nantyglo and Blaina Hospital to have my tonsils taken out. Uncle Noel took me in with my mother on a Sunday night. On the Monday, along with a few other children, I was prepared to have them out. We didn't have any idea what the op was all about, but one by one we went from the ward into surgery. The next thing I remember was waking up some time later to discover my throat had been cut. I was looking forward to ice cream and jelly, but all I was given was toast. I couldn't wait to get home, but unfortunately, that was only the first of many operations to come in later years.

That same year, my brother got a job in County Hall, Newport. County Hall was the headquarters of Monmouthshire County Council. It was deemed a good job to work there. In the October of 1953 Graham had to go back to the army to do a fitness course, but on returning home just before Christmas he came down with a very serious illness. Graham was sick with TB, a very infectious disease. My mother, father and I had to go to Blackwood Pontllanfraith for x-rays and I also had to have a skin test to see if we had any developing symptoms. Luckily, we had none. Graham had to be confined to bed with medication for some time. In April of 1954 he was sent to Glan-Ely Hospital in Cardiff for an operation and recovery. Graham eventually came home, but it wasn't until March 1955. In the time he was in hospital, my father visited him on Sundays, catching a bus from Ebbw Vale to Cardiff every week. My mother always did the same on Saturdays; sometimes her brother, Uncle Noel took her by car. I went on occasion too, but I couldn't go in to see him because of the restrictions.

Graham couldn't work after he came home for another year, and it was quite a strain on the family. In that time, I had failed my 11 plus, and in 1954 aged 11 I changed schools. Children from the Rassau usually went to Glyncoed Secondary Modern School, but because there was overcrowding that year, they sent our year to Willowtown School in Ebbw Vale instead. It was a lot further away than Glyncoed School where we would've normally gone to. They provided a bus from our local garage to take us, but it turned out that it wasn't unusual for the bus to be late. Sometimes there would be no driver to take us, or they couldn't get it to start, and occasionally they'd forget to pick us up when it was time to go home. It was a bit of a traumatic time for me around these years with all the things going on, but I got by. Looking back, it made me stronger for what was to come.

Starting in Willowtown School in September 1954 was an experience in itself. One because we were strangers to all the other new starters, and two because we were bullied as we came from the Rassau, and the other students thought we shouldn't be there. Willowtown was a very old school. The school was not far from the town of Ebbw Vale. The main building was a large hall with classrooms surrounding it. It had two extra classrooms built in a large play area and some way from the main building was a large block of extra classrooms that housed the science, woodwork, and cookery school.

It took some time to make new friends. The first day I had to be taken to the Headmaster's Office because the ritual of sticking pins in the new starter's bums went wrong when someone badly scratched my leg and blood was drawn. It didn't help that I had short trousers on. The class I was assigned to, 1C, was the lowest one could go. The teacher was Mr Graham Bull, a man I have hated all my life. He took an instant dislike to me and was on my case daily until one day the red mist appeared in my head and I called him carrot head. You can imagine his response. There was no going to the headmaster in those days; it was instant punishment. Two canes across my right hand that I can still feel to this day. The only consolation from this was getting moved out of the class. I was moved to class 1B at Christmas.

We soon learned that at morning break time there was a ritual that was handed down in the boy's yard. Everyone would congregate by the one gate entrance and boys of all ages would run out, down the hill, and across a fairly busy Road. You would keep running down and across to a bakery. When you got there, you'd buy a loaf of bread called a batch which cost you four pennies (in old money). You'd then sprint back and fight to fend everyone off who tried to get some of your bread. Obviously, the older boys and the prefects were the main contenders. This bread was red hot, and it wasn't unusual for teachers to check student's desks after a break as sometimes you could smell fresh bread in the classrooms.

I continued my education in 2B the next term. In May 1955 I turned 12, and my father had a very bad accident at the colliery he words at in Ebbw Vale. At the end of his day shift one of his fellow work mates shouted to him that they were ready to finish and that they should get ready to walk the long way back to the pit bottom. My father shouted back that he just wanted to get one extra lump in the top to finish and fill his dram. As he hit into the big lump of coal, down the whole roof came - down with a roar! He was completely buried. Luckily, his mates were quickly on the scene and dug him out. It took some time because of the danger that more of the roof could fall in, but after some time he was pulled out and taken to hospital. The doctors found he had fractured his pelvis, ribs, and head, along with some other facial injuries. It was a very big shock to my mother when the men came to our house to break the news to her. Over time, he recovered very well, but when he was eventually well enough to go back to the pit, he couldn't go underground to work. Instead, they gave him a light job on the surface. He also suffered with nightmares of the roof falling from the accident.

1956 came around without much change. I was still holding my own in school as an average student. My failure to pass the exam to go to Ebbw Vale Technical School was disappointing as it was an all-boy's school, and they were big into woodwork and mechanical engineering. At that time, I started to spend more time away from my own street and spread my wings around the other streets in the Rassau. I started fishing as there were a lot of ponds about, mainly feeder ponds for the Ebbw Vale steelwork which at the time employed about 11,000 men. My mother never let me go out without the stern warning about where I was going and about the dangers of ponds and fishing. It also worried her that I had just had a new bike, something she never wanted me to have, as I was quite reckless. I also started to get more friends. I started to play football with a group and with boys who had gone to Glyncoed School a year bellow and above me. Going to Willowtown School didn't do a lot for my year. A couple of friends and I who had a big interest in football started to send letters to clubs in the English First Division for programmes and autographs.

1956 was also the year my father took over the stewardship of Ty Bryn Working Men's Club. He had been helping out behind the club alongside working at the colliery. The club had just got a loan from Webb's Brewery, Aberbeg for £27,000. This was a huge loan at the time. It was to rebuild the club and as the club got bigger it became the best night out in the area. Minibuses came from as far away as Swansea just for a night out. My mother called it a den of inequality/inequity.

After my father took over the running of the club it got bigger and more popular. At one time they ended up selling something like 32–36-gallon barrels of beer a week. This was 1957 and beer was one shilling and three pence for a pint - that's 8p today. I also had a job on Saturday mornings. I would get the barrels ready and clean the cellar for the drayman who would be fetching up the beer for the week. As I said, the club had borrowed the money to rebuild itself from Webb's Brewery. Therefore, we had to sell their beer and spirits, but we could have one guest brew and we were allowed four barrels of Rhymney beer a week. Rhymney beer was a better pint and my father kept most of that aside for the locals. We lived about a quarter of a mile from the club and my father would walk on his own with the sometimes-large takings at 11:30p.m. in the dark. As I said earlier, the road up to our house only had houses and streetlights on one side too because of the Cwm Nantmelyn Brook. My father would do this late-night walk for a long time, until the police heard that there was a hit on him being planned. A man was arrested and confessed to planning a robbery, but luckily, no incident ever occurred. We moved from Rhyd-y-Cae into the club soon after this.

It was around this time, that I was began showing an interest in girls. Boys back then would wander around shops, or the town centre and girls did the same; hoping you could get to chat to someone and get a date. Some friends and I started to take a great interest in Cardiff City Football and journeyed to Cardiff a lot to support them. It was a long train from Ebbw Vale to Ninian Park Halt, and another home after the game. My heroes at the time were the great Welsh players John Charles, Trevor Ford, Cliff Jones, etc... I also went to a rugby international in Cardiff with my father, but I had to sit in the car for an hour on the way home so everyone else could have a pint in the pub.

I had been going to a snooker hall since I was 13 years of age. You had to be 14 to use it, but the manager Parker Wallace was the type of man who had the sense and thinking that it was a way to keep young boys off the roads, and so he allowed us entry. There were three very good snooker tables and one that was a little bit ropey; we always made the new boys play on that one. It was always warm, and for six pence you could have a game and a fag. Two of us would play and the loser paid for the game.

In early 1956 my mother and father had a big decision to make. They were asked to move from our house to live in the flat that had just been finished in the Ty Bryn Club. We were asked because of my father's job at the club, but it wasn't one of the most secure jobs in the world. Because of this, and as my mother was a big chapel person, she wasn't very happy about the move. I, on the other hand, was very excited at the prospect of living in a club though. It was decided we'd make the move. I was very sorry to leave Rhyd-y-Cae because we'd be moving away from all the friends and neighbours surrounding us. I'd grown up living there for the previous 10 years, and I was going to miss them and the memories.

Moving into the club coincided with me leaving school at 15 years of age, something I was very pleased about. The prospect of getting a job in

Ebbw Vale around that time was very good, especially if you had a family member working in the steelwork… which I didn't. I had a great interest in horses and thought about becoming a jockey, but it was deemed that I would grow too tall. I was also interested in carpentry, and I knew the builders working on the club, so I was cheeky, and worked my way in there. I finished school on Friday the 8th of July 1958 and started work on Monday the 11th of July 1958. I was never a big boy. A large physical stature was never a phrase used to describe me - not at 15 years of age and standing at about 5'10" tall. I also weighed only 8½ stone wringing wet. This meant that the building game was very tough for me, but it was all I wanted because it was where I longed to be; outside in the fresh air, although it wasn't so great in winter. Fifteen years old and there I was: apprentice carpenter by day, part-time barman at night.

The building firm I first started with was TC Charles and Sons from Beaufort. Two brothers ran the firm. They were builders and undertakers. Eddie Charles, the elder, was the boss. He was a very dower man. He had the face of an undertaker, ginger hair and didn't suffer fools gladly. His brother, Wyndham, was a very nice guy; very understanding to a young boy just starting out in the trade. At one time they had seven men working for them, and they all knew their jobs. I was mainly with carpenter Bob, whose real name was Richie Lewis - that's Wales for you.

I worked with different trades while at TC Charles and Sons and gained a good knowledge of the building industry. The first job any boy had to learn was to make the tea, which in those days was a work of art. In those days the water was boiled in what was called a billy can. It was a tin can with a wire handle and the lid of it also doubled as a cup. This can was filled with water and placed on a paraffin contraption called a Primus stove. You had to light this thing to provide a flame. Then, you had to keep the flame going while you boiled your can of water to make the tea. Every week the tins and cans had to be cleaned with wet sand to get the tea stains out of them as there was no hot water those days. At 15 years old you soon took the rough with the smooth working at a building firm, whatever the weather. In my early days on the building site there were no power tools, so everything was done by hand, blood, sweat, and tears.

My first week's pay in 1958 was £2 and 10 shillings. However, in some way of a joke my stoppages and fees came to £3.00! I somehow owed the company! The men I worked with, like a lot of men at that time, liked to have a pint at lunchtime, and it wasn't long before they allowed me to do the same. One Saturday morning after work, I got so drunk that when I got back home, I had to climb over the roof to get in. We were still living in the club, and I did this because I didn't want my mother to see the state I was in.

Living in the club was having a big effect on both my mother and father. My father drank too much while trying to keep tabs on dishonest staff and club accounts. My mother continued to go to chapel and from there worried about our future at the club. Soon after we moved to the flat above the club, my mother saw an opening to make some cash for herself. On Saturday evenings, the club was always a full house. She thought to try to make some money, she would start selling hot dogs to go. This turned out to be a goer! Big time! With the help of some ladies, it became a big hit with the punters. She got a good deal on sausages from a local butcher and rolls from a baker. She charged £1.00 each and couldn't make enough of them! Soon there were ham and cheese rolls flying off the bar on Sundays too. She saved the money she made from this and when we eventually left the club under strange circumstances, she was able to put money down on a new house where my brother still lives.

Apart from cleaning the cellar for my father on a Saturday, my other perks were collecting glasses near the stop tap and getting rid of pints that were left on tables. I would put the dregs in a couple of white buckets and tip the liquid into beer shorts. Anything left on the tables went down into the cellar to be filtered back into the barrels with some special ingredients. After this was done, I would wander through the club looking for dropped cash around the chairs. A good place to look was in front of the bar. There was a slight gap where money would go, and any spare coins were good pickings.

In the summer of 1960, I went with some boys on holiday to Butlins, Pwllheli. One of my workmates organised it with a trip from Tredegar. What a time we had! One of the boys was a good singer and we formed a bit of a group, calling ourselves Freddie Bell and the Bell Boys. It was the start of the swinging 60s, drink and girls everywhere. It didn't take long for me to lose my virginity there. I came home wearing a scarf to try to hide the evidence, but it was no use. My mother caught me, and to her disgust my neck had so many love bites on it you would've thought someone had tried to hang me!

In the autumn of 1960, an old friend asked if I would do some work for him. I took this opportunity to get experience, but he soon realised I was very green. It turned out I wasn't learning a lot about carpentry with TC Charles, so I finished with them and started with Aplin Bros - a decision I would make again as it set me up for the rest of my working life. I always had a good personality and got on well with my workmates. At Aplin Bros, the two brothers had been my neighbours when I was young in Rhyd-y-Cae. Harry had become a very good carpenter, and he also liked to do a bit of plumbing, so as his apprentice, I got very good as time went on. Around this time our position in the club became perilous as my father was accused of mishandling the club funds and faced the sack. My mother was distraught about the fact that these people could accuse my father of all the corrupt dealings in Ty Bryn. The situation was saved by the fact my mother had put her savings down on a house down the road. For a deposit, my former boss, Eddie Charles, used his connections with an estate agent to get us a mortgage. So, we moved from Ty Bryn into Glan-y-Nant. I was in no position to contribute to the mortgage as I was earning very little, so it was up to my brother, Graham, to take on the mortgage. It was £106 per half year. He also got my father a job with the council at the local waterworks.

My mates at this time were a motley crew: Ray Jones, Gerald Williams, Robert Herrage, Mike Meredith (Nipper), John Jonson, and a few others. We would drink in The Rising Sun in Beaufort, a rough pub to say the least. We'd play 3 card blind brag, sometimes winning fairly, and sometimes by cheating. When we weren't doing that, we'd go to the Queen Ballroom Tredegar to look for girls. Drinking underage wasn't acceptable, and the police were likely to come into pubs to try to catch us boys. In The Rising Sun, the landlord, Arthur, would tell us to deny that any drink in front of us was ours. He would back us up and say we were waiting to go to the boxing club downstairs – great man, Arthur, one of the old characters. Before the pubs were officially open on Sundays, we would go to The Castle Inn at the top of the Rassau. It was owned by Horace and Gwyneth Norman, and their helper was Tom Bruin. It was the place to go for an illegal drink. They called it Drinking Boulters – probably after the fishing line. About 15 to 20 men would sit around in one room. You couldn't sit down and have a drink because it was illegal. You'd sit there with no drink in front of you and then every 10 minutes Horace would shout "Next!" This was the cue for four men to go into the bar where four half pints of beer would be lined up. The men would bolt them down in one go and then go back to the room to sit down. The call went out for the next four men to come up, and round and round you'd go. This would go on for some time. As one can imagine it didn't take very long to get drunk out of your mind! As youngsters we loved to get the old men bladdered. When it was made legal for the pubs to be open on a Sunday in 1961, Sundays were never the same again in some ways. Before it was legal, some people used to organise trips to England, just over the border, just for a Sunday drink.

Through drinking in The Castle Inn, I got involved with some new friends. As it was at the top of the Rassau, on the border with Tredegar, my new friends and I always went to Tredegar to dance. It just made sense to make friends with the boys at The Castle. It was also on the edge of the moors and a huge open mountain space. I got involved with the men who kept mountain ponies in that area and spent many hours on horseback in the mountains, keeping an eye out for our ponies. As I mentioned before I was into horses quite a lot. A couple of us boys would get a few horses from a horse breeder. We would break them in for riding, and then he could take them and sell them to riding schools. He'd then fetch more for us to ride and break in, and the cycle continued. I even got a couple of small ponies of my own. Sometimes we had problems with boys from Tredegar. They would come over and steal the horses to ride. We would have to go over and recover them, sometimes with force which resulted in my nickname, the Sheriff of the Rassau!

One Friday evening in 1962, my friends and I were having a drink in The Castle. One of the locals suggested we needed a haircut. So, one of the local contractors, a man they called Farouk, borrowed some hair cutting tools from the landlord, and with the great amount of persuasion of a few pints, he started to attack our heads. Now my friend, Curley had a mop - as his name suggested. Myself, I had the traditional Teddy Boy style, long greased up hair with long sideburns. When Farouk had finished, we were completely bald; not something young men aimed for in those days. When I arrived home that night my mother burst into tears when she saw me. "What have you done you stupid fool!" she said. My father was more to the point and said, "If you think you're staying in this house 'til it grows back, you've got another thing coming." To make matters worse, the following morning I had to go to have a smallpox vaccination as there was an epidemic raging in Wales. The same day my friend Willie had to pick his mother up from Abergavenny Mental Hospital. I went with him, and when I got out of his van, he locked me out. I had mental health patients following me around the grounds.

At the start of 1962 I was not very happy with my job. I was working on my own in a big house in Brynmawr, doing a carpenter's job and not getting what I thought was a fair wage for it. On my birthday in May, which was my 19th, I didn't get the raise I was expecting, so I decided to look for another job. My friend, Nipper Johnson was working for a firm, Drury Construction in Sirhowy, Tredegar. He told me they wanted carpenters, so I went over to the site and asked the site manager for a job. He looked at me and asked was I tied to the film I was with. As I wasn't, he said that although I looked very young, he would start me as an Improver Carpenter. This meant I had doubled my money immediately. I went back and told my boss, John Aplin where to stick his job. He was not very pleased. Time to move on Gary I thought to myself.

As it happened the carpenters that had been working for Drury Construction had gone to a big building site at the Rassau above where we used to live in Rhyd-y-Cae. I managed to get by as there wasn't a lot of technical things to do. After a while, a carpenter started from Aberdare, Brian Beacham - what a great guy! He immediately took me under his wing, and I learned more in three months with him than I had in the previous three years. He coached me on the goings on at big sites. Not long after Brian moved on the site, our work there came to an end, so I had to look for work elsewhere. Still only 19 years old, I took to the Rassau site. They had plans to build 250 houses in 12 months, so a lot of carpenters worked there. The main contractor was Wilson Lovatt, a firm from Wolverhampton. The carpenters were under subcontract by Griffiths & Smith.

In October 1962, I started with Griffiths & Smith Carpentry Contractors. The way they paid you meant there was no guaranteed wage. There was a price for everything you did and that is what you would get paid. They took tax and paid a stamp. It was called piece work. In the first few weeks I found it very hard, but I was lucky that there was a carpenter who I'd started my trade with in the roofing gang who had just finished the roofs. This was the time when for a boy to become a man you had to stand up for what was yours around you. If you weren't careful someone would come into the house where you were working and steal some of your materials, or do an easy job in your house and book it in. I wasn't a big lad, but I did have a loud voice, and that was definitely needed on occasions. I soon made friends with other carpenters, and we looked out for each other. We'd eat our food together in one house and stuck with each other.

Come Christmas that year, 1962, we had a white Christmas. What we didn't know at the time was that on Boxing Day we were going to have a blizzard that would start a very severe winter. There was a hard and long frost. I finished work two days before Christmas and due to the weather, I didn't start back at work until March 1963. I had to sign on the dole as the site was completely closed. I went from earning £15.00 a week to £2, 17 shillings, and six pence dole at home. Our house was the only house around with running water at that time. Everyone else's pipes had frozen solid. I earned a few bob carrying water to other people's houses. My best customers were Mrs Gibson and Auntie Annie in the Red Lion Pub just across the road from ours. She paid with beer and fags. Clearing snow was another earner but sitting in a pub making a pint last a long time became a bit boring. Even when we did get back to work in March, things took a long time to get fully back to normal. Some of the former carpenters returned, some didn't. I got together with one chap, Keith Morris, who was a very quiet chap. He was a little bit older than me and had a very good apprenticeship with Charlie Price, Abergavenny.

Around the spring, my social life took a dramatic turn when one Saturday night a young lady came into the Castle Inn and caught my attention. She seemed very smart with blonde hair. As lots of my close friends had girlfriends, I thought it was about time for me to get to know more about the opposite sex. It didn't take long for me to chat her up and arrange a date for the following Monday at the Astoria Cinema in Ebbw Vale. When I got there on the Monday at the arranged time, I had forgotten what she looked like as there were a few young ladies who looked alike. I quickly apologised to her and made a joke of it. I suppose I fell hook line and sinker for this new way of life, and I soon met her parents. I had my reservations about them. As she was an only child, they were very protective of her. At that time, I don't think I was the boy they had planned for her. In the summer I went to Blackpool with a gang of boys and ended up with a tattoo of the girl's name on my left arm. When I came home my mother raised hell. She cried, "What if you marry someone else!?" She always spoke the truth, and she was right.

Later in the year, I was still working with Keith Morris, and we were offered to do some work on some bungalows. We were tasked to put the roofs on. The chap building them wanted to start that weekend, but we didn't have our tools with us. So, we went onto the site where we had been working at the time and broke into a house to get them. Unfortunately for us a watchman, who should've realised who we were, reported us to the police. The next thing we knew the law were accusing us of stealing from the site. They couldn't prove that anything was amiss, but we were told not to return (we were sacked). That didn't matter too much to us as we then got a job immediately with Gee Walker and Slater in Tredegar. That was the start of many years working with Keith. We had a great partnership together. We put the roofs on this site and then another site at the start of 1964. We thought we would get some inside work with Gee for the winter, but like all building work, we were laid off so that the regular carpenters could have the jobs.

Off we went to the next venture – C Price & Sons: Abergavenny, Rogerstone or Newport. Keith had a car at the time, but I couldn't drive so that job didn't last that long either. On our way again. Next up, Modern Builders from Newport to the site in Aberfan, near Merthyr. This firm was not known as good payers, but it was a job after all, and you didn't have to use your car as there was a van to take you wherever you were going. They picked Keith up in Brynmawr and me by a pub in Beaufort. This was the most death-defying experience you could imagine. The van wouldn't stop for you to get on, it just slowed down and you'd have to jump in. This applied to when you got off too. The van would just slow down, and you jumped out. We tried this for a week and then Keith decided to take his car. At one point when we received our pay, we were due to be given a bonus, and when we weren't, the seeds of discontent appeared again. In retaliation, we jacked (a term used quitting in the building trade), but not before our hate for the firm kicked in. We nailed every pipe in six houses out of spite. On to the next job...

In-between all of these job changes I was getting on quite well with my girlfriend's parents. However, one Saturday it all changed. Nipper, Rob Herrage and I had all been drinking in The Castle Inn. Nipper had just gotten a Ford, and he was driving down from the pub after a good drink when he started to mess about. I was in the back. Before we knew it, he had turned the car over and rolled it down the road. I was thrown about and ended up scrambling through the window. I don't know how we all got out, but we ended up trying to turn it upright, which we did. We jumped back in and drove it to a field and left it there. I went home and said nothing. I went down to the girlfriend's later that day, and on arriving at her door I duly collapsed in a heap. Her parents had to attend me collapsed and stinking of beer - not something future son in laws should aspire to.

In April of 1964, my father had a bad heart attack. At the time they called it thrombosis, and we all thought he wouldn't make it. On May 1st that year I turned 21 years old. It wasn't celebrated like it is now. Still, it felt like a big milestone for me, but having your dad on death's door made it a pretty low-key day.

At the end of May Whitsun Bank Holiday that year, Jenny, Nipper's girlfriend and my girlfriend, Joyce went on a trip to Barry Island with some factory from Brynmawr. Barry Island was the place to go in the 60s. On arriving, the traffic was so bad we decided to get off the bus before we'd even got onto the island. Instead, we decided to go into the Ship Hotel, a big pub. At about 12 o'clock it was full of youngsters enjoying the day out and we were happy to join in the fun. By 4 o'clock we had left and were on our way to the fair to get some food. All I can say is we were fairly well-oiled by that point. Up through the fair we went and by strange coincidence Sandra was also visiting Barry that particular day. Her bus was even parked next to our bus. A fight started on our bus and some boys on her bus tried to intervene. It was all sorted out. Nipper and I got off our bus and went looking for a pub for another drink. When I got off the bus Sandra saw me and could remember it when I met her properly two years later.

We went to a pub nearby and it was full and manic, so we ordered two pints each. While we were on our second pint it all kicked off. There was fighting, tables were going over and general mayhem. The police came in and started to get everyone out. They came to us and said, "Out!" I said, "No way. I want to finish my pint." With that along came this big sergeant who said, "Get them out!" In seconds we were mangled and marched to the door, thrown in a van, and handcuffed to a boy on either side. The boy opposite me in the van abused the policeman next to me, so the policeman punched him straight in the face. That was when I decided to keep my mouth shut. That was about 7 o'clock in the evening. We were taken to Barry Police Station and locked up. Nipper was in the cell next to me, and we could talk through a hole in the corner where the pipes came through. I must have fell asleep because after a few hours I called to Nipper, and he didn't answer. I thought they let him out, but he was having me on. I was shouting abuse at the police and wanted to have a pee, but they wouldn't open the door. So, I had to pee in the corner. Around 2a.m. they let us out. When they came to my cell, they said, "What's that in the corner?" I said, "I asked to go to the toilet, but they wouldn't open the door!" This guy said, "You'll have to wash the cell out." I told him, "Do it yourself!" He immediately locked the door again, only for me to ask for a mop and bucket to clean the cell.

We were let out and told not to remain in Barry or we would be back in a cell in no time. We had been charged with drunk and disorderly, and refusing to quit a licenced premise. We started to walk home, which is about 34 miles from Barry to Ebbw Vale. We'd gone about a mile when a car came down the road. Taking a chance, we thumbed the car and it stopped. The boy driving asked where we were going. Tongue in cheek, I said Ebbw Vale and he said he was going to Blaina, and it was no problem to drop us off in Beaufort. What a bit of luck, the first we'd had all day.

The outcome of this mishap was only just beginning. We decided to get a solicitor and had to go to Newport for someone to take it on. As a result of that particular day at Barry Island, the place had started receiving bad press with headlines saying that young people taking over the island. When we saw the solicitor, the first thing he said was for us to get a proper haircut, for me to shave off my sideburns, and if we had an older brother that we were to wear his suit and a proper shirt. Then, he said we should get our girlfriends to say we hadn't had a drink all day and that we were respectable couples. The day of the court case came just three weeks later with us looking completely different. As the other cases rolled out, we were very concerned as they were sending some cases down for prison. When our girlfriends gave evidence, they both said exactly the same thing and said it like they were singing a song – it didn't look good.

When the bench was considering the verdict, they were eyeing us up and down. Overall, I think the solicitor's advice to us was spot on. However, the verdict was guilty as charged. We were given a £50 fine which in 1964 was a lot of money. Plus, we had to pay the solicitor so all in all that one trip to Barry Island ended up being a very expensive day out.

By the end of May 1964, I had already worked for four different firms; that's how I lived my life. Nothing seemed to worry me, but I was very concerned about my father who was now not very well at all. I was still working with Keith Morris, and we had a good friend of mine, Robert Herrage with us as a labourer. We went together to the Heads of the Valleys Road which was a big job. It involved being a shuttering carpenter, which was something I had never done before. Keith knew a little bit about it, and it wasn't long before I got into it. Going to work as a shuttering carpenter was a big step in learning about carpentry work. Shuttering involves building a length of retaining wall in concrete. You take a large section of rock and clay out of the ground. Then form what's called a kicker to butt the large shutters against (which were 8" by 4" lumps joined together to make up the length of five metres). After that you bolt all these bits together and then pour wet concrete in to form a wall. The following day, you remove the shutters to reveal your new concrete wall. You could earn good money doing this type of job, but typically you had to work long hours – 10+ hours a day, seven days a week. It was heavy work, shuttering big walls and bridges. You came across all kinds of men too. There were a lot of Irish, Scottish, and a lot of men they called travelling men who lodged in local houses or in caravans, but as the saying goes the craic was good. I worked there until October when they went quiet for the winter and let us off.

I still had a girlfriend, Joyce, and got engaged to her around this time. Also, my friend Nipper got married to his partner, Jenny. I was persuaded by my girlfriend's mother to buy a house with their help. We got one not far from where they lived which was a bad move. It was £1000, which was a good buy in those days, but not long after the house purchase things between us changed.

At the end of the job on the Heads of the Valley Road, I had purchased a van off a man I was working with, and I learned to drive. I hadn't passed a driving test, but that didn't bother me. I got another job with Gee

Walker and Slater again, but this time in Bargoed. I was pleased I had my own transport and had left my friend Keith who had become a foreman on the road. In one of my not so clever moves I had rowed with my Joyce, and she had ended up walking home. That particular evening was after a few pints, and I had decided to go to her house to have it out with her. This was the wrong thing to do. Her family wouldn't answer the door, so I took to hammering it with my fists. They still wouldn't respond, and so that was it. One girlfriend lost; one house gained. This wasn't something I was proud of either, but lessons would be learned. I suppose I should've learned my lesson already from when we had tried to run away together on a previous occasion and failed. I didn't make any contact with Joyce after this for a long time and realised it was over.

In March 1965, after a brief job back with Aplin Bros, I started work back on the Heads of the Valleys Road. This time I was working with Ted Perry, Sandy, a Scottish lad, and an old guy called Bill Willard who was accompanied by his dog, Spot. Keith was still there too as a foreman and was very good at his job.

One night when I was in the Red Lion a young lady came in to buy something over the bar. I was having a pint with some friends, and she had auburn hair and looked very smart. I always had an eye for good looking ladies, and as she was leaving, I followed her out. I made a little conversation with her and asked her out for a date. This began my time with Margaret. I didn't realise she lived not far from my house, and she was the youngest of three girls. She had a very possessive mother, but a nice family. We started going out at regular times. I now had a better car, a mark 1 Ford Zephyr, which had 6 cylinders and a bench seat. It was a flying machine, no good in the hands of an idiot like me. We visited her sisters in Underwood and Caldicott, and together we went out with Nipper and Jenny. She had a collection of Elvis records which we used to listen to. The only problem I had was with her mother. When we were in her front room her mother would barge in every half hour to say something, or sometimes when we were outside in the car she would creep up to the side of the car. Because I was working long hours on the road I sometimes went to sleep when I met her; her mother found that strange.

In August that year I got itchy feet again and Keith had fallen off a bridge on the road. I wasn't in the radar of the foreman who replaced him, and we didn't get on, so Ted Parry and I jacked and went with a friend of mine Jim Touhig (Jimmy) to work with the firm Charlie Price, Abergavenny. The job was in Ponthir - new houses there. I met a carpenter, Arthur Manning who was a good guy. We all had a good working arrangement together. Later in the year a carpenter started there called Derek Ball and when I gave him a lift home to Pontypool one night, he mentioned that I should come over to the Garn Rugby Club for a night out. That conversation may have been the catalyst for the biggest alteration in my life.

After Christmas 1965, the site was finished, and we were transferred to Abergavenny on the Mardy. The minute I got there I knew I wasn't going to get on with the agent straight away. His name was etched in my brain in a second. I was putting a set of stairs in a house one day and he walked by and told me to turn my small radio off as he didn't allow radios on his site. When it snowed heavily in the Rassau and I couldn't get the car out, he refused to pay inclement weather money. He was pleased to see me finish there in March 1966 and I was pleased to leave him, but I had to part company with Ted Perry. From that job he went onto the building of Neville Hall Hospital, and I went to work for an Irish subcontractor, Paddy Maher in Beaufort, working on some bungalows.

As I was now working on my own, I was struggling to put roofs on. There are a lot of two-man jobs in carpentry, so I was on the lookout for a carpenter to help me. I thought of Arthur Manning who came to the last job with us. I went down to Pontypool to see him, but he had given up site work to go in the factory, Saunders Valve, as a maintenance carpenter. I gave my old pal Keith a call and as he was only renovating a bungalow he had purchased, he agreed to give me a hand. It was nice to work with him again. When we had finished the roof, Keith went back to finishing off his job and I jacked and went to work with Taylor's Treforest.

I got engaged to Margaret on Christmas that year, but she was starting to become a bit possessive. She accused me of seeing someone in Pontypool. In reality, it was when I had gone to see Arthur Manning, but that was the straw that broke the camel's back. She offered me the ring back which I took with great relief, and it looked like I was on my own again! Not long after I finished with Margaret, I started to go to the Red Lion opposite our house more often. I got friendly with a lad called Alan Davies who was also single. We went out quite a lot. On Thursday nights we went to a pub in Tredegar, The Lion, which was on the main street. A band would regularly play there, and they sounded good. We got talking to them in an interval and they told us they were playing the following evening at the Garndiffaith Rugby Club. So, the next night when we were looking for somewhere to go, we decided to give the rugby club a look.

Not being familiar with Pontypool, we had to ask a few people how to get there, but we found it eventually, and we were quite surprised and what a good night we had. We picked up two girls in the end, local girls. One was from Penygarn and one from Wellington Road. We went out with these girls for a few weeks, but after a while I think they got a bit fed up. We went back again a few weeks later, and it was that evening that changed my life forever.

By June 1966 I was 23 years old, and it had been eight years since I had started work. I had been employed by 16 different firms. I had been engaged to be married twice, and I was in a difficult position with the house I'd bought that I no longer wanted to be in. At this time, I was at a crossroads of my short but hectic life. I was considering a change of scenery or venturing into the outside world. Maybe I'd go work abroad, or at least outside of Wales. Fate, however, would lead me in a different direction. My life was planned out, but when two girls came onto the floor for a dance one night, something switched and kicked into overdrive.

There was something about the girl with dark hair that stood out. "I'll have the big lump," I said. I asked her for a dance. Something about her told me I'd have to get to know her. After that dance I tried to chat her up, but she seemed a bit reserved. Her and her friend went into the lounge part of the club, and we followed. We could now see they were with another girl, and two into three won't go. We asked them if they wanted a lift home. They said yes, and it wasn't long until the end of the dance, so we took them to my car. Obviously, I didn't know where they lived, so Sandra, the girl I fancied, sat in the front, and showed me the way.

It was quite the experience driving from Garndiffaith to Penygarn in the dark, after a few pints, and having rarely been to Pontypool before. We dropped the one girl off in Penygarn after I clipped a car with my mirror on the narrow bit of Leigh Road. Then, we came up to Torfaen Terrace and Sandra told me to turn right. I had to turn the car around Afon Llwyd Terrace and ended up just parking it around the corner. Her friend Diane got out and disappeared around the back of River Row. Sandra was wearing a very smart grey skirt and a white blouse. I tried to put my arm around her to have a little peck, but she pushed me off. I thought what've I got here, and the conversation didn't flow either. I had served my purpose, taking them home.

Then someone appeared in front of my car: Sandra's mother. She'd been on her door and was looking out for her and seeing her in my car, came to see what was happening. Next, she went to look for Diane and got her back in the car. I dropped Sandra off at what is now our house and said I would see her again on the following Monday 7p.m. by the horseshoe. After that, I dropped her friend off on St Luke's Road before heading home.

Come Monday I was looking forward to meeting Sandra again, as our first encounter was very brief. As I am always very punctual, I was outside the horseshoe before 7 o'clock, and there was no sign of her. After about twenty minutes I drove up the road trying to work out where I had dropped her off. Then I went up and turned by the Pretoria. While turning I spotted the boy who I had worked with two years back, who had originally told me about the Garn Rugby Club. He sat in the car and wanted to know what I, an Ebbw Vale boy was doing in this place. I told him about the date I had and that she had not turned up. He said he knew of Sandra and played darts with her uncles. Not being one to be let down without good reason, I wanted to know why she had stood me up. So, we went to the Garn again the next Friday night. Sandra and her friends were there, and I had a dance and made conversation to inquire as to why she let me down. She said she thought I wouldn't show up. I gave them a lift home again, but this time I just dropped them off outside her house and said I would pick her up the next night, Saturday at 7p.m. for a date. She couldn't get out of it this time! So, on Saturday I was there outside her house at 7 o'clock and out she came.

After all the past problems with girls I was nervous, but the date with Sandra blew all the problems away. I knew this was something special. For some reason, and I don't know to this day why, I took her somewhere I had never been before, and have never been to since. It was over towards Blackwood and up to a place called Markham, a pub called The Carpenter's Strange. We had a meal, something she had never done with previous boyfriends, and in another moment of great change in my life I told her my name was Gary, and I have been Gary all our married life.

Part Two

My Life With Sandra

Sandra Mary Vann was born 19th May 1942. She lived with her mother, Marion Vann née Coles, and her father, William Bill Vann, who I unfortunately never met as he passed away in September 1965 with a heart attack. Both William and Marion had come from large families local to Pontnewynydd and Varteg, a village just outside Pontypool. Bill's family all lived in Pontnewynydd and had worked in the local steel forge. Sandra had a stepsister, Barbara, who lived opposite her house. Barbara was from William's first marriage. His wife had died suddenly some years before he met Marion.

When I first met Sandra's mam, who I ended up calling Ma, I took an instant liking to her, as she did to me. She had a very warm and understanding personality. It was sad that I only knew her for such a short time as she would have loved to see the wonderful family we produced. Sandra and I got on like a house on fire. I took her to places she didn't know existed. In the July after we met, 1966, the Football World Cup was being hosted in the United Kingdom, so I decided to take Sandra to London. I was always an adventurer but had never been to London on my own before. In fact, I'd only ever been to London once; going on a pub trip to see Howard Winstone boxing for the world championship. After that, the only part of London we saw was the inside of a pub. So, off we went. We took the train from Newport and sat in First-Class. When the guard came to check our tickets, our Second-Class tickets didn't match the First-Class compartment we were in. In those days, the carriages had a long corridor along the train with compartments off it. I had to pay the extra cash for the First-Class seats. Meanwhile, Sandra had gotten out of her seat and went down the train warning other passengers that the guard was on his way. When he left us, the corridor which was full of passengers was empty – good thinking Sandra!

We arrived in London about 11 o'clock and thought we might see the changing of the guard at Buckingham Palace. I hailed a taxi. "You can't do that!" Sandra shouted. The Valley girl came out of her straight away. When we arrived at the Palace, we were too late for that guard, but we went onto Horse Guards and saw it there. After that, it was a quick trip to Westminster Abbey. Because it was the World Cup there were a lot of crowds and groups of people going into the Abbey. My quick thinking clicked on – why not join a tour group to get a free look around? Sandra knew nothing of my plans and hadn't been with me long enough to know what I was like. We joined a group of Japanese tourists, and we were just counted in. Sandra couldn't get over how I knew my way around. Truthfully, I was blagging it; I didn't know anything!

I had been told that Lyon's Corner House was as good a place to eat as anywhere else for lunch. So, we made our way there and found a seat. We ordered our meal, both Sandra and I had the steak. We sat there for quite a long time, and everyone seemed to be getting served but us. Being a little bit shy, I asked where our meal was, only to be told we were in the wrong restaurant. We had been sat in the fish restaurant and nobody realised. Anyway, that didn't take long to fix, and we were served soon after that. Later in the afternoon we were going to go to the wax museum, Madame Tussauds, but it was closed. I was struggling to find somewhere else to go to. We could either catch the 6p.m. train from Paddington station and get home about 9 o'clock, or we could go somewhere else and catch the 9p.m. train home later.

Sandra has never been one to make big decisions, but she said she would like to go to the Underworld. She thought the underworld was the underground. She really meant she wanted to go to Soho. That's where people went in the 60s; the place was busting. It was the start of the permissive society, strip clubs, and porn shows. There were big bouncers on the doors to pubs with old honky-tonk pianos. When we passed a pub, Sandra wanted to have a look inside like it was the Royal Oak. She was disappointed everything wasn't underground.

We got back to Paddington for the 9 o'clock train home. We got into our carriage, and there was a no smoking sign on the window which Sandra tried to remove with a coin, but the station guard was watching her outside. The trip home took a lot longer than normal because the train at that time of evening went via Gloucester. It was called the paper train. We arrived in Newport at 1a.m. after a very long ride.

Throughout that summer I took Sandra all over South Wales. She seemed amazed that I knew so many places: Porthcawl, Barry, The Gower, the Monmouth and Gwent countryside. Then, I introduced her to two of my best friends, Nipper and his wife Jenny who are still friends of ours. The evening I decided to introduce Sandra, I called on them on the off chance they'd be in. Unknown to me, my ex-girlfriend, Margaret, was also visiting. When we went in, I could have dropped to the floor, but Sandra being her cool self instantly made herself comfortable. I disappeared down the pub with Nipper just after this meeting, but our next get together was a lot less awkward.

I borrowed a canal boat, and we all went for a day out: Sandra and I; Nipper and Jenny. We went from the Pontypool to Gilwern along the canal and Sandra and Jenny got on like a house on fire. It rained on the way back, so us men got wet to the skin. We called into Sandra's house when we got back with Sandra's mom giving us the usual warm welcome that she always gave.

I couldn't get carried away with Sandra as I still had a house which I had purchased when I was with my ex-fiancée. So, I had to make some arrangements to sell it. Luckily, my father knew someone who was interested, and it was sold for the same price I got it, £1000. I only had to pay for the mortgage payments I hadn't yet paid. Luckily again, my brother came to the rescue and paid it off. Sandra also wondered why I kept the left sleeve of my shirt down, which I did as to not expose my tattoo of Joyce's name. Not long after this, I had the tattoo covered up with a flower. About this time, I also changed my car. I put my Ford Zodiac in for a newer Ford Anglia. Sandra didn't like the new car and preferred the old one.

Just after I started seeing Sandra, I finished working for Taylor Construction and had started back with C Price Abergavenny. My old friend Jim Touhig, a good mate and a very good carpenter had a big shuttering job starting in Monmouth and wanted me with him. We had a van to travel together in, and the job was going well, but then, on Friday the 25th of October 1966 a disaster occurred in Aberfan, near Merthyr. A colliery tip slid down from high up on a hill and engulfed a local school. It was devastating as the disaster hit just after the children had arrived for their lessons. It completely engulfed the school and killed 144 people including 116 children. The event affected everybody for a long time. The next day in the afternoon the call came out that they needed volunteers to go over to help make the surrounding tips safe for fear of another landslide. I went with some friends. We worked for a few hours before being called away as the tip had been made safe. It was a harrowing experience, and not one to forget.

Looking forward to Christmas that year I started thinking about another engagement. I must've been mad thinking Sandra would take a chance with me after having two previously cancelled engagements. We made friends with a girl Sandra had been with when I met her. Her name was Viv, and her boyfriend was called Colin. One Saturday night we went for a night out in Hereford, somewhere I had been when I was single. It was known as Park Hall Ballroom in Wormelow. It was miles from anywhere, a fair few from Hereford. That said, it was always a good night out. This particular night was very warm, so after a bit of dancing we went outside to cool off. While walking around the grounds I saw this fountain. The heat inspired me to run through it, but when I did, I didn't realise there was moss on the floor of the fountain, and that it would be so slippery. So, I fell headlong into it and struggled to get out – much to the amusement of several onlookers. This "idiot" motif has ended up following me a lot in my life.

Christmas 1966 was soon on us, and we decided to get engaged. Sandra's mam was over the moon. She thought the world of me. Myself, I was convinced that at last I had found the right girl for me. Our plan was to get married the following October. We celebrated our engagement by going to Park Hall Ballroom again. We went on New Year's Eve with Sandra's friend, Vona, and her boyfriend, Steve. We had a great night and at the end of it we looked for some mistletoe to bring in the New Year. I spotted some on the ceiling and Steve, being a very tall chap, picked me up to get it. When I grabbed the mistletoe part of the ceiling came down with it. Bang! What a mess! The manager appeared who wasn't very amused, but what could we do other than apologise for the mess we'd caused? Some chaps arrived and cleaned it up and all was fine. Drinking and driving laws were being set around this time, but alas it never worried me as much as it should have.

In the New Year, 1967, Sandra's mam who had always suffered with ill health started to go downhill and the conditions she had been suffering with were getting worse. At this time Sandra, who had been spoiled all her life had to respond to the task of looking after her. One Sunday, to everyone's amazement she cooked Sunday dinner. It was very good I must admit, but Sandra's mum went downhill fast. She was admitted to County Hospital in March and passed away on the 25th. It was a very sad occasion indeed as she was very well liked by all her family and friends. Everyone she encountered respected her even through her bouts of ill health which she suffered with all her life.

After Sandra's mother passed away, we decided to bring our wedding forward to May, and as it was Sandra's birthday on the 19th, we made May 20th the date. Sandra lived with her sister opposite our house until our wedding, and her husband, Bert, helped me get our house ready for after our wedding. He also paid for our wedding reception. We had a small wedding just close family and close friends. The first night of our honeymoon was spent in the Royal Ivy Bush Hotel in Carmarthen, and the next we were in the Atlantic Hotel, Tenby. Finally, we came back home ready to start married life.

Moving into 28 Torfaen Terrace was quite a shock to me after the easy life I had been used to at home. There was no hot water and a coal fire which had to be lit every morning if you wanted heating. The only toilet was outside and there was no light in toilet. For washing, we had a Belfast sink, and it was a big shock when I had to hand over my wages, but all of these things didn't bother me as I now had Sandra as a wife. I started to make changes and put things how we wanted them straight away. I got an old gas geyser to give us hot water and a bath from some prefabs (prefabricated houses) on Limekiln Road. We fixed it up in the kitchen and then installed it. All these things made life a little better in Torfaen Terrace, but all these changes still left us feeling unprepared when the biggest unplanned news came in. After a few weeks of morning sickness, it was confirmed that Sandra was pregnant.

I had finished the job we had been on in Monmouth, and I parted with Jim Touhig. I started on a job in Ebbw Vale with a lad from Abertillery. We were to refurbish some flats for Stan James Con. It was very good money, but sadly it didn't last long, so, we were off to the next job in Penarth. I also changed my car again from the Anglia to a Ford Consul, 375 model. It was a beautiful car. Meanwhile, Sandra was having a hard pregnancy. After some bad morning sickness, she went for a doctor's visit. They found she had very high blood pressure, so she needed to rest for long periods of time. One morning while heading to work, a car cut across the road coming out by the Horseshoe Pub and damaged my car. Luckily, I was alright, but there was some damage to the front of my car. I was lucky the lad I was working with had a car and we used his until mine was repaired.

I hadn't been married long when I started getting friendly with Sandra's uncles who lived next door. They were Sandra's dad's brothers, all confirmed bachelors. Uncle George had worked all his life in the Pontnewynydd Forge before going to Llanwern to work. Uncle Walter had worked at the Forge too and had since started working with the gas board. He had a very close friendship with the lady who kept the shop opposite our house who he called Auntie Glad. Last but not least was Alf (or Buck as he was known). He took me under his wing and introduced me to his dart friends in the Pretoria Public House which was at the top of the road. He also worked at the gas board. In those early days of our marriage, the local community of Pontnewynydd were very friendly, as everyone knew each other. There were new flats and maisonettes which had been built nearby. All seemed to have very nice people living inside. In the next door down lived a single lady called Edna and her mother Mrs Edwards. They were very friendly and good neighbours. Across the road lived Sandra's stepsister from her dad's first marriage whose mum had passed away when she was very young. Her husband, Bert had been a soldier in World War II. They met while he was convalescing in Pontypool Hospital. They had two children: Geraldine who was five years younger than Sandra; and Joann who was only three years old when we got married.

I had also started to venture into another local pub, The Royal Oak. One Saturday after work I went in. It was just after midday, and there were about eight men in the bar. All were in full voice singing to a song that was on the TV. It was a show for children, Skippy the Bush Kangaroo. As soon as I called for a pint someone said: "You've married Sandra Vann, haven't you?" Yes, I said, to which they replied: "Can you play darts, and what's your name?" When I said Gary, the landlord replied in a loud voice: "Gary Owen up and under!" His name was Garnet Terrel, and his wife was Mary. From that point on, I knew this was my pub!

In September the work in Penarth came to an end and we were asked to go to Cwmtillery to work on a new housing site. Things had only just started and there was no money there. So, we went looking for a job with J.F. Diamond Con. We worked on the Coronation Club in Newport. We had only been working there a few days when Brian, who I was working with, decided it wasn't for him. We split up on good terms and I stayed there. I got on well with a carpenter who was from Caerphilly while Brian went to Abertillery with an old mate. I stayed with Diamond's on a few different jobs. I worked on a bridge in Taff's Well, made signs and a workshop in their yard, and also put up offices on the bypass through Llanwern Steelworks. After Christmas, my old mate, Keith Morris, contacted me saying that he had been contacted by an agent for Diamond who he had worked with to work on a new sewage farm in Llangynidr and Bwlch. I asked if they could transfer me to the job in Llangynidr and I started in the end of January.

Sandra had not been very well at all. She had to go into Cefn Ila Hospital for a rest. In the early hours on the 9th of February, I was woken by Sandra who thought the baby was ready. Up we got and went to the hospital. Later in the morning, I phoned from the phone box by the pavi (pavilion), to ask how she was as she wasn't meant to have the baby for another five weeks. They told me she had been sent to County Hospital, Panteg. I phoned them and they told me I could visit that afternoon. With my mother in Ebbw

Vale and Sandra with no mother, I was in a bit of predicament as to what to do. I tried to keep a cool head and after dinner I went to the hospital. When they let me see her, she was on the gas and air. I stood by the bed holding her hand like I knew what I was doing. "Don't worry," they said. "We're looking after her. We're going for a minute, but she's quite alright." They had been gone through the door for 2 minutes when all of a sudden, the big mound in the bed made a whooshing noise and when I lifted the sheet up there was this baby on the bed! You've never seen anybody move as fast as I did. I went through the double doors like the road runner screaming for a nurse. They came from everywhere and when I finally stopped shaking, they told me I was the proud father of a baby daughter. My mother and father were over the moon at the thought of a grandchild and sad they didn't live a bit nearer. All of Sandra's family were also giving us their best wishes. We named the baby Lynne Mari. As she was premature at only four pounds three ounces, we had to leave her in the hospital until she had gained weight to 5 pounds.

She was born on February 9th, 1968. In those days men didn't have any paternity leave after the birth of children, so it was straight back to work for Diamond's in Llangynidr. To get there I would meet my friend Keith in Brynmawr and one week we would go to work in his van and the next week we'd go in my car.

Sandra's uncle Fred, who lived in the row behind us was a real character. He was very old school and a very big man in more ways than one. He was an elder in the church who liked to drink. When there was a bus driver strike the pickets stopped Peaks' Buses, but he would continue to drive through the picket lines. He was afraid of no-one. His hobby was messing about with old cars and scrap. He would fill petrol tanks and door panels with soil on scrap cars to make them heavier and therefore more valuable when he sold them. I got an old car off him for £5 once – just to go to work in. I would take the tax off my good car and use it when I was travelling to work, hoping the police wouldn't stop me. The problem with the old car was that the brakes weren't very good, and you had to pump the pedal when you wanted to stop. The car lasted me for quite a few months until coming home one Sunday afternoon going through Cwmavon a new car I was following stopped quite suddenly. I pumped the brakes hard, but I hit the back of the car. It wasn't hard and there wasn't a lot of damage, but the driver got in a pretty state. I said I was insured, and I would sort it out, but when I went to my insurance broker, they told me the Craven Insurance Company had gone into bankruptcy and they would not be paying out. That was the last thing I wanted to hear. I didn't do anything for some time, hoping the driver of the car I had hit had forgotten all about it. No chance. I received a county court order against me for £60. £60! I didn't have £6 to spare! I went to see a solicitor, Everet & Tomlin. I paid a £5 fee for advice. He said offer to pay 10 shillings a week, which the driver accepted.

The job with Diamond was finished, so we went to work for two carpenters in Caerleon. It wasn't very good, and we only lasted three weeks. When they paid us, we had to have a cheque, but I didn't have a bank account. Sandra asked Auntie Glad in the shop if she could change it for us and she gave us the cash. From that job, we went to a job in Nantyglo, near Brynmawr. It was for a new comprehensive school. It was with a firm from Rogerstone called Hinkis & Frewin. They had to be the worst firm I've ever worked for. This was in September and from sub-contracting all year, we had to go back on the books for this job. Because I was back on the books and I didn't have a tax code, I was made to pay emergency tax which was a big chunk of what I was supposed to be earning. What didn't help was that it wasn't a very good wage to start with. The site was also a bad one. It had been an old coal tip and we were up to our necks in muck: being in the dirt; shuttering ground beams; and working in the rain. It all resulted in not very good craic on the job. To make matters worse, while going to work one morning, coming up through Cwmavon to Blaenavon I went around a bend and there was a van parked on the curve. As I went to go around the van, a car came down the road. I braked hard but went into the back of it.

When I got out two men appeared out of the van. "Why are you stopped there!?" I said. They said they'd run out of petrol and one of their friends had gone to get some. "Why weren't one of you warning traffic coming up the road?" I said. We exchanged details and I had to get my car back to the pavilion garage for repairs. After a few days I had a letter from this chap's solicitor trying to claim for the day's work for these men. It stated that because I had run into them, they had lost a day's work and the contract they were going to have. I immediately wrote to my insurance company stating that if they were so concerned to get to work and secure a contract, they would've made sure they had enough petrol in the van for the day. I didn't hear from them after that. However, now without a car, I had to catch the bus by the post office to Brynmawr every morning for a job with a rubbish firm.

All these incidents were building up. I couldn't pay the county court money and HP (hire purchase) on my car. Also, other bills were coming in and we were struggling big time! Sandra's uncle Eric asked me to have a chat with him about our finances. Our problem was we were paying out more than we had coming in. In a few weeks, after I got the car back and my tax was sorted out, I got a job on weekends putting in some fascia boards and soffit in Griffithstown. This helped us out until Christmas. News came on our site that a big job was coming up in the New Year, 1969, in Brynmawr so things were starting to look up.

1968 had been a trying year to say the least. After Christmas we went back on the job at the school. We worked for a week before we jacked. We started on our next job in the first week of January for Costain Con. It was going to be a factory for RCA, an American company that made compact discs for the music industry. When we went over to the site on the top of

Blackrock, we were amazed at what was going on. Contractors had just finished two single storey buildings for offices with an entrance in the middle. On one end was a big part which held the clock-in station. I had never had to clock-in or clock-on at a site before. A little way down the road was a large car park which would hold about 300 cars. The site of the factory was at an elevated position with a concrete ramp for access. On the site were stores, drying rooms, a carpenter's workshop, etc. The whole area was flooded with light from tall scaffolding towers, and they had generators supplying the power. This firm meant business and to get this job done. Again, it was wet and cold as it was January, but the money was excellent! There were plenty of oilskins to wear and they had people come around the site with hot soup. There was a canteen with ladies cooking all day and they had a drying building which was brilliant to keep your clothes dry. The hours were long – 10-hour days, seven days a week, but as I said the pay was excellent.

All that said, I came very close to getting crushed one afternoon. When I was drying my gloves on a compressor, one of the lightning towers blew over in the wind and landed just a few feet from me. The cables on it hit me flat to the muck on the floor. It was a close shave indeed! The factory was in this part of Wales because it had the cleanest air in the country. The job would last ten months. All the men and contractors got on very well, and every six weeks all of the men went out on a night out to relieve the pressures of the job. The main agent, a New Zealander, was a great man. On one night out in Newport, one of the boys in the club said to me as we were leaving to hit a fire extinguisher. He knew that in my drunken state, you didn't say things like that to me because I was guaranteed to do it. When it went off the hose was going everywhere. The rush for the door took it completely off its frame. Nobody was amused. The next morning, we were down at the club to repair it. Another night I was drinking with a different guy. We were on black rum, not something I was used to. I ended up crawling up our road from the pavi and was in bed for two days.

As the year went on, we had to arrange to work what they called "nighters." I was to do work and not interfere with people who were working in the day. I was in charge of a team of lads. We discovered that if we worked hard until about 1a.m. we could then get some sleep in the sheds or on the job. If you didn't get some sleep, it was awful because you had to work the next day again. It could be very difficult, but I soon got the hang of it. When we had a night shift coming up, I would put some boys on a shift in the day. That way we were already getting everything ready for when the normal shift finished at 6p.m. We would get into top gear and the job would be done by about 11p.m. I would drive my car over to a car park on a different road and go home. Then, you'd get up at 5a.m. to get back on the job before anyone starting at 6 o'clock got to work. We got away with it and no-one knew anything different.

In the spring of 1969, Sandra said she might be pregnant again. It turned out she was. Our Lynne was just over 12 months old and was still very small. We were worried for her, and I was also very worried for Sandra after being so ill with Lynne.

Prince Charles was made Prince of Wales in the summer and a job with Costain Construction looked like it was going to finish around October. Sandra hadn't been too well at all, and I was glad when I could get from work to be with her. When the job finished, I tried to sign on the dole. I had a small job I could do in my own time and the dole money could've helped support us as I helped out more at home, but they kept sending me for jobs I didn't want. I tried to sign onto the sick, but the doctor wouldn't have it. When Sandra had to go into hospital with toxaemia and high blood pressure, I asked her sister if she could look after Lynne for a few hours a day so that I could do a bit of work, but she said she had to think about Joann. So, as a last resort I had to take Lynne up to my mother's house for a few days so I could get some money in.

In November I managed to sign on the dole by saying I would take a job they had offered me when my wife had a baby. Sure enough, another girl arrived on November the 25th who we named Ceri. Lynne was 19 months old when Ceri was born. Now with two babies, we agreed a rota for how we'd look after them. In the night I would see to Lynne who now was in the small bedroom, and Sandra would look after Ceri. That backfired on me because from a very early age Ceri would go to bed at 7p.m. and not wake up until 7a.m. I started work with I. J. Caddick, a Blaenavon firm who wanted two carpenters; Keith Morris, my friend, started with me. It was a very small firm with a very closed shop atmosphere. Everyone was always watching one another. It was very cliquey, and the money was rubbish, so started to work just subbing for them. Keith went to a joiner's shop to make windows, and I went to the Arthur Jenkins home in Blaenavon. It was mainly a bit of fixing: door frames, skirtings, etc. I just blasted on like as if I was back on price work. The other carpenters didn't know what had hit them.

Come February in 1970 a job came up in Panteg Steelworks from Douglas Construction, Swansea. They were going to build a new pickle line and a new arc furnace. It was shuttering work again. When we started, the site was bare. Our first job was to erect the office's canteen and store buildings. A lot of the time we didn't have much to do, so we would wander around the steelworks which made special stainless steel. The steel was made using argon arc furnaces. There were three 15-ton furnace pots which were filled with mainly scrap metal, and a few other materials. Then, three giant rods lowered down onto the lids of these pots and electric charges would start the steel making process. When we started to work, we had to shutter a big, long tank called a Pickler, which would later be filled with acid. The acid would "pickle" the steal to remove the impurities. Once again, the work was seven days a week up until Christmas 1970.

Sandra found out she was pregnant again in June. It was quite embarrassing to think we would have three children in three years. In July, on my brother's birthday, July 2nd, my father passed away. He had been quite ill for a number of years, and in my mind, we were lucky to have him see me happily married with two children, and unknown to him we were having a third. Sandra struggled on with the children even though she didn't always feel up to it with her blood pressure.

Come October, we started shopping early in Cardiff for presents for Christmas in case Sandra had to go into hospital again. The baby was due around Christmas time and 2 weeks before Christmas Sandra was admitted to County Hospital. With a bit of luck my mother and her sister, Auntie Carrie, came down to look after our Lynne and Ceri so that I could go to work to get some wages. Lynne was two years and 9 months. Ceri was 13 months old. It was some task for the ladies as Carrie had never had children and my mother's last child was me – something she would never let me forget! Sandra came home on Christmas Eve and had to go back in on Boxing Day. The baby was born 30th of December – surprise, surprise – another girl! We named her Helen. When Sandra went back in on Boxing Day, I thought I would make the old kitchen look a bit brighter. So, I started to paint which was a difficult job to do when I also had to look after two small children. I hadn't finished it on New Year's Eve, so I had to work through the night because Sandra and baby were due home the following day. When we left the hospital the top nurse in the maternity unit called me into her office. She said it would be dangerous for Sandra's health for her to get pregnant again, so would I mind seeing a consultant about getting sterilised in the near future. OK, I replied.

Sandra coped very well with the extra baby considering all three were under three years old and there was very little hot water in Torfaen Terrace. We still had to deal with the outside toilet and coal fire, but we were very happy.

It was back to work in the New Year (1971) in Panteg Steelworks. The boys I had been working with got itchy feet, so we jacked and moved onto a job at the top of Cwmbran above Fairwater. It was on a huge concrete tank that acted as a reservoir. It held water for all the high-level housing in Cwmbran. All the big shutters had to be handled by a crane. It wasn't that hard, but it was quite cold, and we had to have a lot of heaters around us to keep frost off the concrete. This job was for Shepherd Hill Construction.

In February I went to see a consultant about getting the snip (sterilised). He explained that once it was done, I wouldn't be able to father any more children, and that if I married again, I'd be firing blanks. No problem, I thought. So, I signed to have it done on the NHS. I soon received a letter to go to the County Hospital to have the snip. Not knowing a lot about the job, and not having anyone to ask, I just brought clothes for an overnight stay. The letter told me to bring that and didn't say much else.

When I arrived, someone said not to worry, that it's just like having a tooth out. I was taken to a ward and told to get into a bed. Later a nurse came and asked a few questions. She asked if I had shaved. Rubbing my chin, I said yes. She smiled and said, "down there." Then I realised she meant down below. "No," I said. She replied, "I'll help you do it later." She left and a little while later a male nurse came with a razor and helped me out. My op was the following day. I was told to have a shower beforehand. No problem, I thought, but when I tried to wipe myself down, Sandra had given me a new towel that hadn't been washed. Red dye from the towel came off turning my skin bright red. The only thing to do was to have another shower and wipe myself down with my t-shirt. Then, when I put the pyjamas that I'd brought with me on, they were so big that they could've fit someone twice my size. I was only 9½ stone and as there were no mobiles in those days you just had to get on with it. When Sandra came to see me that evening, she informed me the pyjamas were my brother-in-law's. He was about 14 stone at the time. Anyway, the following day after all the chaos, the job was done, and I was allowed home.

Once again, I was moving on in work. This time it was to RDR, a firm from Pontypool who had a job for me in Tredegar. We knew the foreman well and he was going to look after us. We only worked there a few weeks and found it difficult to get the money they owed us. So, we all finished and split up. I went with a boy from Blaenavon and the other two went over the valley to look for work. After this, the next job was with my mate, Gary Howells. It was a multi-storey car park in Ebbw Vale town centre for a firm from Cardiff. We were constructing the deck on the fourth floor, but again there were many problems. So, we moved onto the next job which was land reclamation after the Aberfan disaster. Our job was to make the coal tips safe. We were shuttering culverts and water outfalls. Around this time, I had to provide a sperm sample to see if my operation was a success. For this, they provided you with a small test tube you had to put your sample in. While attempting to do this one evening Sandra started to giggle. That was the end of that.

We got there in the end, and everything was alright – the operation was a success. Since we'd been married, our closest friends remained Nipper and Jenny Johnson. They came to our wedding and since that day while we had had the three girls, they had had three boys. We went everywhere together. Our first holiday was to Butlins holiday camp in Minehead in 1970. We couldn't go on the Saturday because our Ceri had measles. We left her with my mother and went on the Sunday. On Monday morning, we rang my mother to see how everything was and it was plain to us to see she was struggling to look after her. So, myself and Nipper drove back to Ebbw Vale to fetch our Ceri, much to Sandra's relief. In the early days of Butlins holiday camp we went full board. The chalet was very small and the toilets and washing facilities were opposite where we were staying. The camp was an excellent place for children as everything was free.

In the autumn of 1971, while I was working in Caldicot, our Ceri was taken ill with sickness and diarrhoea. She was admitted to St. Woolos Hospital. It turned out she had a very contagious stomach bug, not much luck for Ceri around this time. Once the doctors discovered what was wrong, we had to take Helen in too to make sure she didn't have it as well.

In the early 70s, I had become a bit of a local at the Royal Oak Pub and had begun to make a lot of friends from going there. There were some larger-than-life characters there: Arthur Lewis, the butcher; and Roy James, a bricklayer; Nev Taylor, Malcolm Hobbs, who was a lot older than me; and his lovely wife Margaret, who had moved into the new houses that had been built in Pontnewynydd. It was a very good community to live in and be a part of. One of the boys suggested I might like to join "The Buffs," a secret working man's organisation, the full title of which was: The "Royal Antediluvian Order of Buffaloes, Grand Lodge of England." It was similar to clubs like the Freemasons. I joined the secret lodge called the "Duke of Wellington, Number 3083." I joined on Monday 29th of November 1971. We had weekly meetings in the Pretoria Pub, every Monday evening. There were a lot of local chaps who were members. We would often go to local Buffs lodges and enter sports events: darts, cards, and skittles.

At Christmas in 1971, my old friend Keith, who had started some work subcontracting asked us to help him out on a job, which we did. Later on, I went to work with him on a regular basis. Being self-employed meant there were plenty of bits of work about, and for the first time since being married I was only working five days a week. That was a big relief and great help to Sandra with the three children.

In 1972, we had a lot of work in the Caldicot and Chepstow areas. We were paid good money too. We went to Butlins again on holiday, and this time, we went with friends from just up the road from us, Pam and Neville Taylor. We had a great time again.

When I got married, I started to watch Pontypool Rugby Club. At that time, they were struggling to get a good team. By 1972 though, they were beginning to turn things around. Ex-Pontypool, Wales and British Lions player, Ray Proser had come on board and turned the side around with captain Terry Cobner. They built a team that became invincible for well over a decade. I followed them everywhere. Those were great days to be from Wales, as they were becoming the best side in the five nations, winning everything.

In 1972, the building industry had the first strike in its history. The unions wanted all the workers to join so they could stop the practice of sub-contracting. Being self-employed, as I was, was called "working on the lamp." This was because a lot of the builder boys didn't pay tax or "stamps" – the insurance used by self-employed workers at the time. A lot of the boys were on the dole or sick pay too while working to make ends meet. The strike lasted a few months, and it was not unusual for men called "flying pickets" to come onto your site and force you to stop working. This happened to me and Keith just once in Nantyglo. We walked off in solidarity as most working men did at the time. This working man solidarity was big back then – if one of you had a problem with a boss and jacked, other workers on the site would leave with you.

Around this time, I got myself a small van. It was a Vauxhall Viva with a seat in the back which could fold down. The kids loved that van when we went to Longleat safari park. The monkeys wouldn't come on our van as there was nothing they could pull off, unlike the cars with chrome strips on the side.

Christmas started in the first week of December that year when we were coming home from Caldicot, and a Christmas tree fell off the back of a trailer ahead of us. I stopped the van and managed to get it in. When I came home, Sandra said, "Bit early, isn't it?" As we were having the house renovated, we had to put it up in the front room. In the weeks leading up to Christmas the needles kept falling off the tree. Every day there would be less and less needles. By Christmas Day, the tree was bare. As I've mentioned, the house had continuously been in the process of being done up ever since we got married. The house had been owned by a local colliery company and they had never done any repairs. Our local council, Pontypool District Council had purchased all the rows of terraced houses and had acquired a government grant to renovate them. The Conservative government also gave us the right to buy them, which we took up. It was a gift at £7,850. I had altered our house to suit our children. We had knocked the two back bedrooms into one and the girls had the big bedroom in the front.

In February 1973, the chaps in The Buffs had organised a trip to Scotland to see the rugby international. What was my first trip to Scotland, soon became the first of many. We were to stay in Gullane, a small village some 15 miles from Edinburgh. The hotel we stayed at, The Mallard, had been recommended to us by someone in Pontypool. Having not been there before, a lot of us had no idea what to expect. We started off very early on the Wednesday. Unknown to us, the village of Gullane was of great significance in the world of golf because the Muirfield Championship course is in the village. The Mallard Hotel was not that big, but we had a very warm welcome from the owner, Mrs Clarke, and her family. We arrived at about 6p.m. and she had prepared an evening meal. We sat down and had soup to start, and then a fish course. Malcolm Hobbs, a very good friend of mine said to me "Where's the chips with this fish?" I replied, "They don't have chips with fish in Scotland. Eat some rolls with it instead." Next up was the main course; a beef dinner and finally a sweet to finish. Most of us had never had food like that before. I explained to Mrs Clark that just two courses would've been ample for us. The following morning, she had arranged a trip to a distillery for us and every evening we obliged by drinking the bar dry and having a great singsong.

We headed into Edinburgh on Saturday. In those days you didn't need a ticket, you just paid at the gate when you went to the game. I was amazed at the great bank that surrounded the field which the crowd stood on. There was only one stand which was for prepaid ticket holders. I had trouble seeing the start of the match, so with one of the boys we climbed up the scaffolding where the TV cameras were and watched Wales lose from there. The journey home was something of a disaster. The owner of the minibus had been drinking all night and was not fit to drive. We drew lots and I picked the short straw, so I started the drive, and changed with someone else later; not a very good trip home at all.

When I arrived home from Scotland, Sandra was distraught. One of the children, Ceri, had somehow climbed up onto our fire guard and had taken some tablets that were on the mantlepiece. Sandra went over to the Royal Oak for the landlord, Garnet Terrel. He told her when I left for Scotland that if she wanted anything she was to come over for him. He took her to Pontypool Hospital, and they pumped Ceri's stomach to retrieve the tablets. Thankfully, Ceri was okay.

Work was going well. We were still working in Caldicot for two builders. Some bricklayers we knew told us they might have work for us in a place called Trelleck. Some London businessmen had purchased an area of farmland to build some very big houses. It seemed to be a very suspicious situation from the start and in the end it all fell through. From the pub in June a few of us who worked together went to watch the Epsom Derby. I wasn't a horse racing man myself but fancied the day out. Most of the lads were racing fans and knew about racing, but I was the one that bet on the winner of the derby and had a free day out.

Pontypool rugby was off to a flying start in 1974. We were beginning to develop a big name in the world of the game. The captain of Pontypool who was a good friend of mine got his first cap for Wales. He had been overlooked for some time, but now they were starting to see how good Pontypool RFC was. On April 1st, Pontypool played a game and after having a drink in the club, my friend, Nev Taylor gave us a lift home in his van. It was a van like mine with a seat in the back. Nev Taylor was driving the van with Mike Teage in the passenger seat. In the back was John Perkins – a Pontypool rugby player, Malcolm Hobbs, and I was in the middle. Nev decided to go up through Churchwood to avoid any police. Going up the track, he came to a fork in a lane. He left it too late, and undecided on which way to go went straight into a tree in the middle. In the front, Mike's head slammed into the front fascia. In the middle, I went sliding forward. My legs went under the driver's seat which fractured my ankle. When we all got out of the van, which was now buried in the tree, Mike had disappeared. I couldn't put my foot to the floor. Perky Moore carried me back to the rugby club. Mike, in his panic, with blood running down his face had run back to the rugby club where someone had called for an ambulance. Mike, Nev and I were taken to the Royal Gwent Hospital. Mike was patched up with a few stitches. My fractured ankle was put in plaster. Nev was breathalysed and Mike's brother came to take us home at 2a.m. The next day, it was back to the hospital for a check-up. I was told I would have the plaster on for 16 weeks which was not something I wanted to hear. The plaster was all around my ankle an up to just under my right knee. I had to sign on the sick, something I had never done before. I knew I had some sort of self-employed benefit, but it was not worth the paper it was written on. I couldn't drive for a while, but the boys were good with a couple of pints here and there. Garnet, from the pub, would often shout to me as I came past the wall by the pub. Quite often it was "Gary you've left your fags behind!" and he'd give me 20 Embassy. What a good guy!

After I broke my ankle, the first thing we had to do was to cancel our holiday. We were going to Butlins on Barry Island and just before I had the car accident, Helen, who had just gone three years old, developed whooping cough. It was a terrible thing to have. Helen was ill for three months with the worst cough that you can imagine. It was so bad that a doctor was called out to her. The doctor said he had never heard or seen anything like it. For three whole months Helen carried a towel around with her to catch the mucus which came up from her chest. The only way to describe it is it was like glue.

Meanwhile, I was getting around the best I could with the plaster on my leg. I even managed to drive my van. One day a friend, Malcolm Hobbs, asked if I could take him to get some tomato plants. We went to this garden centre, and I asked if I could grow tomatoes anywhere. Yes, he said. Grow them in buckets if you want. From then on, the gardening bug had been sewn. Four plants came home with me that day. I knocked the side of my shed out. Garnet, the landlord of the pub gave me some glass and I had half a greenhouse with some compost. I was away. Someone suggested I dig a bit of the garden up to plant some runner beans – that was done. However, it resulted in me breaking the plaster halfway down my leg. I tried washing the plaster, but I ended up having to go down to the Royal Gwent to ask if I could have a new plaster put on. "We don't do that," they replied. "We'll just put more on." So, they put more plaster on top of the old plaster; that slowed me down a bit. When it started to crack again, the boys down the pub stapled it up with jungle tape.

For Christmas in 1974 & '75, a few of the Pontypool rugby players came to our local pub, the Royal Oak, for a drink and a singsong with a lot of us local supporters. One such Christmas, we had a tie auction there. Everyone fetched ties they didn't want, and we swapped or sold them on for charity. On this Christmas, Terry Cobner said I should come down the rugby club that night and give the players and spectators some entertainment. We went and when we got there, he gave me a plastic bag. When I looked inside, he had given me one of his Welsh rugby jerseys. I nearly fainted. Instead of heading into the Royal Oak, I took it home immediately. Even when

I got home later in the night, I still couldn't believe my eyes. I wore it to bed that night. What a gift from such a great player!

When the day arrived to have the plaster removed, I drove myself to the hospital. They put me on this table and produced an electric saw. They proceeded to cut through the plaster and with one crack it fell off. "That looks very good," the male nurse said. He went out of vision behind a screen, and I waited some time because I thought someone would come and tell me something. After about 20 minutes the nurse looked around the screen and said "What are you doing here? You should've gone some time ago." When I tried to stand up, it was just about impossible. I hopped on one leg to get to my van, which thankfully, wasn't parked that far away. With a little bit of effort, the strength soon returned. I received a letter to go to physio but being self-employed I had to get back on the job as soon as possible. The girls were growing up fast. Lynne was in Snatchwood School, where Sandra had gone, and she was being taught by the same teachers too.

Christmas came and we were glad when 1974 was over. 1975 was with us and one of the contractors we were working for said he'd secured a job to build 30 houses and more in the coming year. He asked if we thought we could handle the work. It sounded good to us because it meant we wouldn't be moving around, just staying on the same site. I would be starting in the summer, so in the spring of 1975 we planned for our next trip to Scotland. We wanted to be a bit more organised than the last time, so we hired a minibus, but this time we made sure to have our own driver for it. The match was a special occasion because it was to be played on Saint David's Day, March the 1st. Also, there were going to be four Pontypool players playing: Charlie Faulkner, Graham Price, Terry Cobner, and Bobby Windsor. The day had to be spent in the pub to celebrate this. I got a large white sheet, cut it in half, painted the colours of Pontypool on it, and added their names in each corner. This was done in my living room with the carpet rolled up as to not get paint on it – yet, even given my precaution, Sandra was not amused by the situation.

We left for Scotland with one of the best bunches of chaps I have ever been with. All the women were outside the pub waving us off and the two oldest members sat in the front of the minibus for our epic journey. The toilet was a large tundish connected to a pipe that led out of the door of the bus. We stopped for breakfast at the other side of Birmingham. When we got near the Scottish border, one of the boys wanted to go to Dumfries. He said he'd been before, but we ended up getting lost. We tried to go up through the Scottish Borders to get to Gullane, but in the dark we didn't have a clue. We got to the hotel at 7p.m. after a 12-hour trip. However, we received a very warm welcome once again from Mrs Clarke and her family. It was straight into the bar for a good old Welsh singsong and some a few Scottish arias.

The following morning, we went to North Berwick, a beautiful little town right on the sea. It was only a few miles from Gullane and after a good whiff of the fresh air, it didn't take long for someone to suggest a livener. So, in the nearest pub we went. As soon as the locals heard our accents another singsong erupted, good old Celtic hospitality. Come the day of the match, Saturday the 1st of March, it was all systems go. Everybody was up for it, and I was lucky enough to have stand tickets along with two others. The rest of our group were on the bank as it was pay at the gate – just like last year. They were expecting a very big crowd, but the crowd turned out to be even bigger than they thought.

The boys took our Pontypool banner and we expected to see it waving in the crowd. As we walked down to Murrayfield after a few pints, you could see it was going to be massive. We got to the ground, and it was frightening. We managed to get into the stand okay, but the crowd on the banks ended up practically standing on the touchline. I didn't see our banner as there were too many people there. It was way too full to have a drink after the match, so we went back to Gullane. We lost the game 12-10, but that didn't matter to us as it was another excellent trip to Scotland. The total attendance at Murrayfield that day smashed records with an estimated crowd of 104,000; a number that took almost twenty-five years to surpass when Australia faced New Zealand in 1999. We had another great night out in The Mallard after the match which went on into the early hours with many of the locals joining in. There were some rough looking Welshmen having breakfast the following morning, and a lot of sad goodbyes. When we left for home, we left our banner behind as a parting gift.

The day before we left home for Scotland, I had asked the girls what they wanted. The men on the trip usually brought something back to give to the women who stayed at home. To make it easy for me they said "Dad, get us some wombles." They were all the rage at the time. When we went into Edinburgh, me and my friend, Eddie Teague, walked up and down Princes Street looking for these wombles. We finally found them in one shop. They wrapped three up in front of me no problem. When I went to pay, the cashier said "£81 sir," to which I said, "That much for a bloody womble!" The cashier tried to argue that they were talking wombles. I only had that much on me to last me until I got home, and with no credit card back then, back on the shelf the wombles went. I came away with three Girl's World head things instead. They were heads you could put makeup on and do their hair. Buying presents was always a problem when going away. When we came home, our girls put their toy heads in the front bedroom window which had the woman opposite our house knocking on our door. She thought our girls were watching her.

In 1976, we started work on the site we had been given in Rogerstone, near Newport from MRC construction. Mike Towel was the owner of the company. We had done a lot of work for him for a number of years. The job started well, and we were earning £100 a week which was a lot of money back then. When Keith and I started working together some 13 years previous, wages were only £20 a week! The summer of '76 turned out to be one of the hottest summers on record. There seemed to be a nationwide drought. In September, we went on holiday to Barry Island, Butlins to make up for when I broke my ankle. It might be local, but Butlins is the same everywhere. There's always plenty for children to do. This year the boys in the Royal Oak Pub had started to save to go to France for the rugby in 1977. Robert Parry (Patchy) and I organised it. We got underway on the 14th of February with a party of twenty men. There were a mixed bunch. A couple of boys had never been out of Pontypool, let alone been to Paris before.

We flew from Cardiff and had only been up in the air for five minutes when the captain came on the mic to say we had to land in Bristol as there was something wrong with the plane. When we landed, we bumped along the runway, and some of the boys wanted to get off. No-one told us what was wrong, but after some repairs we were off again. We arrived in Charles de Gaulle Airport banged up and shaken. We were taken to our hotel, which unknown to us, was in the middle of the Pigalle, the red-light area of Paris. We were right opposite the famous Moulin Rouge, much to the delight of the younger chaps who thought our location couldn't have been better! The first night we went out to a bar nearby. All twenty of us piled into this empty bar, but by the time we all got a drink it was full of ladies of the night looking for business.

The older members of our group couldn't get back to the hotel quick enough. Meanwhile, the idiots of the party wouldn't go back at all! They wanted to have a look at what was going on. The barman warned the boys to look out for men dressed as women. He said, "They all look the same." We visited Notre Dame, the Eiffel Tower, the Louvre, and took a trip to the Palace of Versailles. We took these trips so we wouldn't drink all day… just all night. I was lucky I went to the game with a few of the boys on Saturday. Wales lost, but we managed the Metro quite well. We were lucky a boy with us, Paul Griffiths could speak French very well, but we still came home on Monday looking the worse for wear.

The British Lions went to New Zealand on tour in 1977. Pontypool had three players included in the tour party: Terry Cobner, Graham Price, and Bobby Windsor. The tour turned out to be a disaster! Things didn't go right on the field, as well as off it. The weather also wasn't kind as it rained the entire time. While they were there, another Pontypool player, Charlie Faulkner, was called up as a replacement; that was a consolation at least. Also in 1977 was the Queen's Silver Jubilee which marked 25 years on the throne. The silver jubilee was celebrated all over the country with street parties. Our celebrations were in the chapel's school room. We had a Punch and Judy and a party for all the children.

In 1978, we were all still working for MRC Construction in Rogerstone. We were now in the second phase of building these private houses which were selling well and kept us in work. This was the first time in our marriage that we could open a bank account. We went with the National Westminster Bank in Pontypool. We suddenly thought we were big now we had a cheque book. One afternoon I came home early to go to a rugby match. I asked Sandra for some money to go out. She said I should go to the bank and get some out myself. She handed me the cheque book, but when I went in to ask for £20, I realised I couldn't spell the word "twenty." Instead, I filled in "ten." The cashier said, "You can have £20 if you want." I said, "It's alright. £10 will do," and that was my first encounter with the bank.

I changed my van for a car around this time. I sold my van to some boy working on our site and the agent on the site was selling his car, so I had his Avenger Estate. It was better for the girls to travel in, and the car was called "Odd," after the number plate. In the summer, we went to Pontins Holidays in Perranporth, Cornwall. Before going, a friend called Colin Hood gave me his AA card in case anything went wrong with the car. Sod's law!

When we weren't far from Perranporth, I felt something go wrong in the engine. When we had booked in and found our chalet, I looked under the bonnet and found oil everywhere. I cleaned the engine up and warned Sandra and the girls that we had problems. We went to Newquay the next day and on the way, I spotted an AA patrol man. I pulled in and asked if he could have a look at the car. I produced my AA card under Mr C Hood, and the patrol man said "Well, Mr Hood, I think you had better look for some other way to get home. I don't think this car will get you back to South Wales. If you try, go quietly, keep the engine clean and filled with plenty of oil, and then you might have a chance."

For the rest of the week, we went to the beach near the camp. When we travelled, we caught the train down to Saint Ives, and on Saturday morning I got a load of rags, paper, and plenty of oil so we could start very early on our slow trip home. We stopped quite often along the way. When we got to the Severn Bridge, we pulled into the services and let the engine cool right down before chancing the trip over. Once we got over, I knew I could get home from there. When we finally pulled up outside our house after ten hours of travelling the old car just ground to a halt. After that trip, the engine had to be completely rebuilt.

1979 saw the end of a very cold winter. Keith and I were still working in Rogerstone and the firm we worked for had been given a job to build a new clubhouse and community centre for Crosskeys Rugby Club. One Friday night in the Royal Oak, a man called Derrick Jones, who went there quite often was asking for a pal of mine to play rugby for a local factory team, ICI. While chatting to him he said to me "Why don't you come along too? We could do with some rugby thinking chaps to help on a Saturday. Tomorrow we're down Barry for a game. Come along. You'll enjoy it." That conversation was the beginning of a life change that went on for twenty years. I joined in April of 1979 and by the start of the 79-80 rugby season I was into rugby big time!

I went to Ebbw Vale for the funeral of the mother of a man I had worked with who was a distant relation. As I was coming near to my mother's house, I thought I would call in and see her. She was going on holiday with her friends "the pensioners" that Saturday. She was in good spirits and looking forward to the trip. My brother, Graham, lived with her. He was forty-six at the time and had never gotten married. He was big into lawn bowls and local theatre groups. I wished my mother a good holiday, gave her a fiver and left. That was Friday afternoon. On Monday morning, my brother rang our house to inform me that mam had passed away on the weekend in Torquay with a heart attack. She had had chest problems all her life but had never been seriously ill. It was very sad. Out of our children, only our Lynne really knew her.

That summer we went to Perrenporth again to go to the places we had missed the previous year. Luckily, there were no mishaps this time. The girls met two girls from another family and this couple kept seats for us every night. The problem I had was that the husband didn't drink like I did. When it was my turn to go to the bar I would down a quick pint on the bar before coming back to the table. Christmas came round and Sandra always made Christmas big for our family, even if we hadn't paid the tax man or bought self-employed stamps.

1980 was soon with us. That summer, we went to Laugharne in West Wales – the place Dylan Thomas made famous. We rented a private chalet from a friend of mine for a week. It was beautiful. We had never been to West Wales before and there was a lot to see and do with Pendine Sands, Tenby and much more.

I finished going to The Buffs as I was too involved with the rugby at ICI. ICI was a very large factory built after the war. It has a workforce of about 7,000. They had a very large club which catered for all sports, and a very large ballroom for dances and concerts. I enjoyed the rugby atmosphere of the players playing at the lower level. It's what is known as "the grassroots" of Welsh rugby. I felt free to let my sometimes-idiotic personality go on occasion. After match singsongs and stupid games were part and parcel in clubs at that level of rugby, but that atmosphere seems to have now gone. Now, the game has gotten more serious and professionalism, even at the lowest level, has ruined the life of the game.

When I first arrived at ICI, they had two teams. The 1st side played at a very good standard for the level we were at. As it was a factory side we were well looked after in the ICI clubhouse. When I started, the chairman was Graham Bishop, secretary was Tom Parfitt, and treasurer was Derrick Jones (Dirky). I fitted in very well. I started with helping Dirky organising the games on a Saturday, and I took that mantle on for all the years that followed. As I progressed to fixtures secretary and then chairman new players came to the club and former players left or became part of the committee. One of these, Graham Morris took over as treasurer, a very good man. However, the thing that benefited the club most for our remaining years was Gareth Cleverly joining. At first, he was a very good player, an outstanding club captain, and he became a great friend of myself and my family. It wasn't difficult to get players in our days at ICI because of the good facilities we had. However, it was always a struggle to get enough players for two sides. Sometimes I'd find myself going into pubs on a Friday night to blackmail the boys to play. When ICI sold the club and moved to be closer to Cwmbran, we were very lucky to make our home in The Old Comrades Club in Sebastopol. Dai and June Vasity made us very welcome there and gave us a room upstairs as a club room. We had some very good players come to the club over the years, too many to name, but the highlights for me were the after-match entertainers, the likes of Piggy Powell and others. That said, the man who let us have our own match day, coach, and the man we could never have done without was Clev.

My social life was the thing that shifted most dramatically at ICI. I was 37 years of age when I started there, and most of the rugby boys were just out of youth or a little younger than me. As I said, I fell in with the after-match activities straight away. I loved the rugby songs and the drinking games; I was into it all. After one evening game, I had a very lucky experience on a coach coming home. Two of the boys were messing about at the back of the bus. I went to try to squeeze around them but got pushed into the window. The whole window went out and I was heading out with it, but one of the two boys grabbed me and stopped me from falling out. The bus was going quite fast at the time. Over the years I've had some great times. I could write another book just on the twenty years I had with ICI, and later with our new name Pontyfelin. I was fixture secretary, match secretary, chairman, and general dogsbody at one time or another, and I haven't regretted one week of it.

Since 1977, Pontnewynydd had been a hive of activity in the summer thanks to Hazel Jeffries and her friends who organised a yearly carnival for all the children. There were still the old houses, buy newly built flats and houses were popping up and brought more people into the festivities. I became a bit obsessed in '81 at winning every carnival. The carnivals entered four different towns yearly and I loved going to them. Around this time, most mothers were quite good sewers, and if they weren't, husbands were pulled in to do the building floats for the carnival. It made good fun and brought the community together, but the designs of the floats were complex to say the least.

We went on holiday in 1981 to a Pontins holiday camp in Brixham, Devon. It was called Wall Park. There was plenty to do: lots of entertainment; and good places outside the camp. In work Keith and I had to employ another carpenter to help us with the site we had going and the new rugby club. The boss at MRC, Mike Towell had given Keith the job of agent on the club. This meant he was running the job and it meant I was with Colin Jones which I didn't mind at all as he was a mate. When they started two more carpenters to help us work on the rugby club, Colin Jones and I went back to the site in Rogerstone.

1981 was the year of the Royal wedding. Prince Charles and Diana Spencer. The local ladies of Pontnewynydd went into overdrive with festivities. We had wheelbarrow racing from the Royal Oak Pub up to the Pretoria Pub. There was a lot of beer flowing!

We went on holiday that year with a big crowd. There were eight couples and about ten children. We had a great week and when one of the boys had his birthday party, we had a wonderful day. We got all the women to have a photo together, but unknown to them, Ron Whitman was on the chalet roof with buckets of water which he poured down on the unsuspecting women. They all went mad. The women were soaking wet, and it started a water fight which lasted a long time… until the security came and said we were making too much noise! It was good, clean fun.

We nearly had a bad accident one night when Lynne and Sharon Young were babysitting the younger children in our chalet. The door to the chalet had closed which Lynne hadn't noticed. She walked into the closed door and straight through the glass. The camp security came and fetched us from the club we were in. It was unbelievable that she wasn't injured in any way, and the younger children sat on the settee had a piece of glass like a sword in-between them. After that, safety glass had to be installed on doors and those types of doors were banned. For the rest of the week the sun shone, and we had a great time.

One Saturday in early 1981, I was having a drink in the Royal Oak with Mal Green and Brian Gibbs. It was very quiet, so we got a taxi to the Comrades Club in Pontypool. I had a few more pints on stop tap and we left the club. Outside, there were police cars parked opposite the club. I wasn't thinking sensibly and in my drunken state, I went over to the police car and as a joke growled at the two policemen. They immediately got out of the car and arrested me. I started protesting my innocence, but I was taken to Pontypool Police Station and was charged with being drunk and disorderly. The police station was only a hundred yards from the club, but I was locked up for the night. Mal Green told Sandra and she rang the police station to ask when I would be home. She was told "He's not going anywhere! He'll be out in the morning!" I attended court proceedings for the incident, but failed to prove my innocence, and I was slapped with a fine of £50 and a warning to keep out of town.

In the winter of 1982, we had a large amount of snowfall, and I couldn't get to work. When we got there, I rang the boss, Mike Towell, and we had some harsh words about the weather. I said I didn't want to work, that it raised my hackles right up, and told him where to stick his job. So, in the middle of the winter, Colin and I no longer had jobs. Luckily, Colin knew a local builder and we survived. When the weather got better, I changed my car for an Austin Princess. We kept the old one for a working car.

In 1983, we went to Scotland again and as always had a good time with Mrs Clark who I got on with very well. She said, "Why don't you and your family come up in the summer for a holiday?" Sandra was overjoyed! She had spoken to Mrs Clark on many occasions, but they had never met. Later in the year, I rang The Mallard and asked if it was alright for us to make arrangements to go to Scotland. No problem.

1983 turned out to be rugby's last year at ICI. The club had been sold to some ex-rugby players and businessmen. We had altered the skittle alley downstairs and turned it into our club room, but they wanted us out. As a final farewell, we decided to go on tour to Corfu with the 18-30 club. They thought I wouldn't make it because I was 40, but I got there!

We went early April, in the first week of the season. We had a great time, but the reps had no idea how to get entertainment going. So, up I jumped with the rugby songs and games. We were almost followed daily for the rest of the tour by other holiday makers. If they saw the rugby boys, they'd follow. One day we hired motor scooters. I had a 125CC Honda motorbike. We took them up in the mountains. Another day, we rode through Corfu town to another resort. Sandra would've had a heart attack if she had seen me.

In the spring of '83 with Scotland coming up money and money being tight, I thought I'd go back to a scam I used to do many years ago: fiddling tax discs on cars. With a razor blade and an old tax disc, I could do a quick swap and make my car look like it was taxed. I was very good at this. One particular afternoon, we were working on Osborne Road when one of the boys said, "Gary! There's a policeman looking at your car!" I went out straight away and said, "What's going on?" He said, "Your tax disc is not applicable for the present quarter. It is the wrong colour. It's green when it should be red. Can you get it for me to see it?" I reached for it from behind the mirror and was about to put it in my mouth to eat it, as to destroy the evidence, but he stopped me. I had to go to court to plead and plead that I was so broke that I couldn't tax the car, but it was no use. I was slapped with a £50 fine.

Part Three

Family Life with Sandra and My Children, Grandchildren and Great Grandchildren

Sandra was excited for our holiday to Scotland in 1983. We left on a Friday morning so we could visit Blackpool for a night on the way up. We stopped at a bed and breakfast; I had booked somewhere on Albert Road. We arrived at about 4p.m. and went for some food before going to see as much as we could. Sandra couldn't get over how expensive it was to go into the tower. We carried on the journey to Scotland the following day and arrived at The Mallard Hotel in the afternoon. Mrs Clark gave us a lovely welcome and jokingly said we would have to do the washing up for our stay. We were thrilled to stay in a posh hotel together as we had only been to holiday camps before. The evening meal was three courses and guests looked at us and must've thought, "why are they and their three kids staying here!?" Gullane was a very beautiful place in the summer with a lovely beach, just like Gower in Swansea. We went with Tom, Mrs Clark's son-in-law to some highland games. We were accompanied by his wife, Katrina, and other members of their family. The girls made a fuss of Katrina's young children. On Wednesday, we went to stay with Katrina and Tom in Edinburgh and Tom took us around. We left on Friday morning to come back via North Berwick and down the East Coast to stay at night with Sandra's cousin in Sheffield, before heading home to Wales on Saturday.

1984 was the kind of year in our lives that some families never want to remember. Something happened that year which would change our lives forever. It was Thursday evening, the 12th of July, and I was attending a slimming club which was held in the local public house. I was sat waiting for everyone else who was coming to attend for the weighing in to see how much weight they'd lost. A friend of mine came running in to tell me that my daughter, Ceri had been in a traffic accident. She had been knocked down by a car which had been speeding on a road nearby. When I got there the police and ambulance had arrived and quite a lot of people were trying to have a look. Ceri was on the floor unconscious. Looking at her lying there was an out of body experience. It was horrifying; seeing someone you love so much lifeless on the floor.

We eventually arrived at the Royal Gwent Hospital. The ambulance crew were marvellous. The policewoman who was on the scene met us at the hospital to help us further. After what seemed like an eternity, we were sent from accident and emergency to intensive care. At that time, there were no cat scans at the Royal Gwent. We had to be transferred to University Hospital of Wales in Cardiff. Ceri had sustained multiple fractures: skull, tibia, fibula, pelvis, collarbone, and cheekbone. After the scan we were returned to Royal Gwent's intensive care unit where Ceri was induced into a coma and put on a life support machine. Sandra and I stayed by her side for two weeks sleeping there and eating there. Meanwhile our other two children were greatly affected by the incident too. Bless them. They were left at home. Lynne was working at a local store and my youngest daughter, Helen, had just broken up from school for the summer holidays. They had never been left on their own before, but they received some help from my brother and sister-in-law. After two and a half weeks Ceri opened her eyes for the first time. She couldn't talk or walk, and they thought that being in a children's ward would be the best thing for her, so the noise of the other children could stimulate her. Neither Sandra nor I could sleep there, but Sandra would arrive at the ward at 8a.m. One morning, as Sandra arrived, she could see Ceri through the window in the door to the ward. Ceri was in her wheelchair with the sister and nurses all around her, and Sandra thought there was something wrong, but as she got nearer to Ceri the sister turned her around so that Sandra could see her. The sister said to her "Now say it." Ceri said "Mam," and Sandra started to cry. Everyone cried; the sister and all of the nurses.

She was later taught to walk and talk her memory was such that she couldn't remember the time before her accident, so her teachers used to bring children from her class in school to help her remember. After six and a half weeks we could at last bring Ceri home. Lynne and Helen were absolutely marvellous with her helping her. They'd talk to her, take her out for walks in her wheelchair and I was truly blessed to have the most wonderful daughters. Lynne, Ceri, and Helen all together at home once more.

Recovery still took a long time. We went by ambulance two or three times a week for physio for around three to four months. We'd go to the Royal Gwent and Eveswell Pool in Newport. After this time, Ceri could walk unaided and went without a wheelchair. She was home taught by teachers for a year as she regained her strength. When she eventually went back to school, she stayed on for an extra year. While all this was happening, Ceri had received 200 or more get well cards. We were helped as a family so much by friends – too numerous to mention, but I feel that I must mention Maureen and John who were stalwarts and truly helped us through. Also, Sandra's friends, the domestics from Pontypool Hospital who used to collect between themselves and pay Sandra her wages. Finally, Wokkie who used to phone from Pontypool Hospital at 8:30 every morning to find how everything was.

Sandra pulled the whole family together through Ceri's accident. I had to go back to work because being self-employed meant the job had to go on. In 1985 Ceri continued to get stronger and with home teaching went from strength to strength. We went on holiday altogether which proved to be the last time we would all go as a family. We went to the Isle of Wight on the ferry going from Lymington. Sandra wouldn't get out of the car while on the ferry and stayed in it until we arrived on the Isle of Wight. We stayed in Pontins Holiday Camp and had a great time. The ICI Club had closed down and we had managed to get new headquarters in the Comrades Club in Sebastopol. It turned out to be a good move. Dai Vasily, his wife June and their family looked after us very well. We also had a new ground in Pontrhydyrun and changed our name to Pontyfelin. I was still chairman and we had very good men with us: Gareth Cleverly, Graham Morris, and a great bunch of players.

In 1986 I changed my car to a Vauxhall Astra and Ceri was doing fine. She now had a boyfriend, Neil Worwood. Our Lynne who was working in Tesco's had a boyfriend, Chrissy Robinson who had worked with me for a while two years prior. We went on holidays to Pontins Camp in Great Yarmouth; Live Aid in Wembley was happening on the day we went. The first night out we went to a bar. The compère came on and started giving shout outs to people from different countries. This guy shouted, "Anyone from Wales?" Up I jumped and shouted "Yes!" I was the only one who got up. "Ogy Ogy Ogy!" He shouted. I replied, "Oi oi oi!" He asked where we were from, and I said Pontypool. "Pooler, I'll see you later!" In the interval, he came over to us and made a hell of a fuss. He was Phil Kingsley Jones. I knew of him as he had played rugby for Blaina and Ebbw Vale. He had gone to New Zealand some years previous, and he was back to do a summer season. From then on, every night we went to his bar, and he always made a fuss of us. When we left on Friday night, we exchanged ties and he gave us a photo of our stay.

On June 21st, 1986, Lynne and Chrissy Robinson got married. It was a pretty rushed affair, but it went off well with the reception at Pontypool United Rugby Club. We were working now on the community centre in Malpas. Colin Jones' son, Shane had joined our work team and he had managed to get a house for Lynne and Chrissy just up the road from us; 6 Machine Meadow. With all my builder friends, we managed to get it in good living condition. More boys were working for us because the previous year we had gotten a big Bedford CF van. We fitted it out with inserts for tools. I liked it because we had an orange light on the top of the cab which made us look important. We also worked in Bristol and when we would get stuck in traffic jams, I would put the flashing light on and go straight by.

As a result of our Lynne and Chrissy's quick wedding on June 21st, our Lynne was soon in Panteg's maternity ward giving birth. On November 15th, I was on edge up at RTB Ebbw Vale with our rugby team, not because of the game (like usual), but about my first grandchild being born. After the game finished, we were back in the clubhouse. I phoned Sandra for any news, but she said to ring back in half an hour. I couldn't wait that long, so I rang back ten minutes later. She said straight away, "you have a grandson, Daniel." I screamed back into the club room. When they saw my face, the whole place went berserk! Next thing, a pint of I don't know what was thrust into my hand and then a few vodkas and then I don't remember what. I don't remember anything until I got back to the house sometime later, but I didn't stay long as I went over The Oak, hit a table full of drink over, and then collapsed to bed. In the morning, one of the boys who had taken my car keys came to take me to get my car back. On the way back from the club, I called in the hospital to ask if I could see my daughter and grandson. I knew they would say only the father's allowed, but I told them I was working away and had been called back that morning, and I wouldn't be home for some weeks. "Go on," said the nurse, as she let me see them. I nearly knocked out our Lynne with the smell of booze on me, but I was the first to see my boy.

Our Helen left school in 1987 and went into further education for a year. Her quest was to become a dentist. I also took on my friend, Mal's boy as an apprentice carpenter. So, the gang had gone up to five. We now had a big job to do in Monmouth converting the Beaufort Hotel into luxury apartments. We changed our old van for a hired one on lease.

1987 Sandra and I went to Malta for our holidays. It was the first time we had been on our own on holiday, or abroad even. We arrived in Malta in the early hours of the morning. The room was beautiful. Sandra had trouble trying to draw the large curtains as she didn't know to look for the pole to do the job. The evening meal the following day was very confusing. We entered the restaurant and all we could see was salad, so we piled our plates with salad not knowing that it was only the starter. The next thing we knew a waiter arrived with the menu for the main meal. The next evening, we could see other new holiday couples doing the same thing as we did. Malta felt very welcoming because almost everyone spoke English and we had a lovely holiday.

Carrying on in the line of holidays Sandra and I went to Corfu in 1988 and stayed in a lovely place in Dassia. We stayed in a chalet and went on a lot of trips. We met a friend of mine who I was involved with through rugby. Ceri started planning to get married in 1989. Helen had enrolled in September in Cardiff Dental School and was at that point working in Cardiff University Dental Hospital. She stayed in the halls of residence when she was 17 years old. When we took her for the first time, the room she had was like a cell. Sandra's heart broke on the way home thinking of where we had left her. Helen soon made friends and still has them to the present day, and the following year she moved in with them to better accommodation.

In 1988 a group of friends from the Royal Oak decided to start saving so we could go and watch the British Lions play in New Zealand in 1993. Eight of us started a standing order savings club in a bank at £40 pay a month. It was a good incentive for me because it made me give up smoking to save. Alas, after two years three of the guys gave up, but five of us carried on.

In January, our Lynne gave birth to a beautiful daughter, Sinead; a second grandchild for us. It felt odd as we had only hit our 40s, but we were lucky to be young enough to enjoy them. In April that year, 1989, our Ceri got married. After a year of planning, she got married in Emmaus Church, opposite our house. My best friend, Gareth Cleverly supplied a coach to take guests to the after-wedding ceremony in the Three Salmons in Usk.

While looking in the Western Mail, I saw a holiday advertised to Orlando Florida in America. It was a trip inclusive of a tour guide with trips to all of theme parks included. We never ever thought we'd get the chance to go to America, so we booked it for November that year. When the time came, we took the coach from Newport to Heathrow and met the tour guide, a man called Joe.

It seemed as if everyone on the trip was from Wales; we were all a friendly bunch. The flight was long, and we got to our motel in Orlando without a hitch. The guide gave us all the information and we had our own coach to take us to the Disney sites. That evening, while going out for a walk, we stopped to chat with a couple who were on our trip. From that chat, we have been friends with Alex and Gloria ever since. They were from Barry. Alex was a builder, and due to this, we were very much alike. Every day we were taken to a different attraction: film studios, theme parks, etc. Part of the stay involved a visit to Clearwater and Busch Gardens, Tampa Bay. It was a wonderful stay and an interesting journey with a great group of Welsh people.

Our flight home was very good until we landed in Bangor's main airport. The airport was mainly for refuelling flights between Europe and the West Coast of the United States. No-one was supposed to get off after refuelling, but before take-off the pilot made an announcement for passengers to fill the empty seats at the back of the plane as we had been loaded incorrectly at Orlando. He said this would help the plane to take off. Everyone looked aghast at the request. I looked out of the window and saw some fire engines coming towards the aeroplane with men hanging on the side in foil suits. I told Sandra "I think this plane is on fire." "Don't be stupid," she replied. The next thing we knew, the pilot gave a message to quickly leave the aircraft.

Immediately after leaving, and having left all of our hand luggage behind, we had a problem. Sandra being Sandra, she was slow to react. She waited for the people in front of her to get out while I went over the top of chairs. When we got to the doors, a lot of men were waving the passengers away from the aircraft. I had gotten off with just a polo shirt on. Bangor Main was very cold at that time of year. I reached the bottom of the stairs they had put up to the plane and looked back at it. The engine on the back tail was on fire. When we got to the main building, we were told we were in Bangor Main and that there were no facilities for passengers as the airport is just a refuelling stop and U.S. Air Force Base.

After some time, they started looking to accommodate all the passengers for the night, as it was getting late. It was older people first, then families with children, and last couples. If you had made friends with a couple you had met on holiday you could double up. We agreed with Alex and Gloria that we would go together. They took us in an authentic American school bus to somewhere in the outback, an hour away. We were taken to a hotel with a room which had two double beds. After having a laugh and joke about our situation, which we made the best of, we went to sleep.

Come morning, after some breakfast, we were to take the school bus back to the airport. We were hoping to see another aeroplane ready to take us home, but the answer to that was no. After meeting with the rest of the passengers, of which there were 400, we were told that they were repairing the engine of the aircraft. It wasn't a happy situation. Later in the day, Alex and I were having a nose around and I saw the aircraft with scaffolding around it and under tarpaulins. We saw our pilot and asked what was happening and when we could expect to getaway. What he said was unbelievable! He asked us if we were plumbers, or if we knew any plumbers within the group of passengers. He said the engine on the aeroplane had a fuel leak and that was what had caused it to catch fire. If we had been plumbers, we could have soldered it, otherwise we would have to wait for a new part which was coming enroute from Boston. He then said if it wasn't ready by 7p.m. his hours were out, and we would have to stay another night. With that, we returned to the rest of the passengers, and there was an uproar.

A lot of people were not prepared to return home on the aircraft. 7 o'clock was approaching and they informed us the aircraft was fit to go. The same pilot and crew were onboard, but a lot of people refused to go. Alex said if the crew were prepared to chance their lives it must be alright. So, we boarded. It was strange. As the plane taxied out all the ground staff seemed to be looking at that engine in the tail of the aircraft. As me made our return journey, we took a completely different course. It seemed the pilot wasn't going too far from land. As we finally landed in Heathrow everyone cheered and clapped. When we went through customs, they tried to get me into the right lane for a bag search. I politely told them "F off! I've just been held up for two days!" Surprisingly they let me through and that was the end of Sandra's flying days for a while.

Around this time with Pontyfelin rugby, we were having an exceptional season. The season of '88 to '89 was the best in our history of ICI and Pontyfelin. As we now know, it was in the fact the best season we would ever have. We got to the semi-final of the Welsh Brewers Cup which is proof of a good rugby side when you were at our level. Group 4: 1st round, Pontyfelin 6-3 Whitchurch; 2nd round, Pontyfelin 10-9 Bryncethin; 3rd round, Pontyfelin 10-7 Nantyglo; 4th round, Pontyfelin 12-9 Cefn Coed; 5th round, Pontyfelin 15-3 Bethesda; semi-final, played in Newbridge, Hartridge 28-10 Pontyfelin. It was amazing to get all the way to the semi-finals but losing so close meant a very disappointing day for the club.

We were working in Usk during the spring of 1990. It was on a school. I was having some trouble with pain in my groin and back. We had also worked on a school in Cross Hands, and while there I fell off a scaffold and injured my left shoulder. I also broke my wrist. Work was good, but we had to pay retention money out of our cheques, as we were the contractors. This kept amounting in value, but we wouldn't be able to reclaim it until the job had finished.

We decided to call it a day. The men working for us were my son in law Chrissy, and apprentice, Richard Green, who wasn't far off from finishing his trade. They went out on their own and I had to consider giving up as I had been told after having x-rays on my hips to give up the work I was doing. After some more scans it was revealed that I had further problems on my shoulder, neck, and several problems with my hips, so that was me finished with site work for good.

In October we were invited to Gullane in Scotland for Lorna and Dez's wedding. We went by coach and this wedding was something different as it was a wild Irish and Scottish wedding. The atmosphere was one of "anything goes." The amount of drinking consumed was unbelievable!

In 1990 Sandra and I went on a holiday to the Scilly Isles. We drove to Penzance in Cornwall and stayed the night there in a bed and breakfast before catching the ferry to Scilly early the following morning. The trip over to Sicily was horrendous for Sandra. She was seasick most of the way, only fully recovering when we finally got there. We didn't know much about Sicily, and we were staying a fair distance from the town of Saint Mary's. It was a beautiful self-catering flat, but a bit too far out. We fell in love with every island we visited in the Isles. It was like an adventure. We took trips by boat and helicopter. This holiday became our first of many visits to this beautiful place. On the trip back Sandra took the advice from someone we met who told her to stay on deck and look up and not down which seemed to help with her seasickness.

In 1991, Helen was doing very well in Cardiff Dental College. She was still coming home most weekends to visit and had finished the BTEC national diploma qualification that the course offered that July. She moved onto the HND (Higher National Diploma) which went on for two years until she left in 1993. We all went to her graduation in Cardiff together. We were so proud. From there she worked at the Three Blackbirds Pub before moving to Birmingham in December 1993, and then later onto Leeds, but we always found time to visit her or vice versa.

In 1991 I was under the care of Mr John Merrick, an orthopaedic consultant for my joint problems. I was also receiving some physiotherapy too. I was now driving a Rover, and we went in it to Newquay in Cornwall for a holiday with Alex and Gloria who we'd met in America. It was not the best of holidays. We had a very small room, but Sandra wouldn't complain. She went out for a walk early in the mornings just to have a sneaky fag. Our Lynne was pregnant again, but we couldn't say much as we had had three children in four years. She had another beautiful daughter born 4th of November and called her Chloe May. I had a new job from September taking Daniel to school and fetching him home. I really enjoyed that as I had plenty of time on my hands which I was looking to fill now that I was no longer working. I still took on small jobs for people that didn't take too much out of me and got more into gardening.

Before we knew it, it was mine and Sandra's 25-year wedding anniversary. Where had all those years gone? We went on holiday for our silver wedding to the Lake District, stopping in Bakewell and visiting different places on the way. Alex and Gloria came with us to the Peak District National Park, and it was an organised tour. It proved to be a much better trip than our last trip to Newquay and Cornwall. We stayed in the Adelphi Hotel in Liverpool and had a tour of Liverpool included in our stay. Sandra had been on one of her diets for a while but had gone to the extreme and looked too thin and gaunt.

We went out with all the family to celebrate 25 years in September. The celebration also coincided with Sandra's 50th birthday, so we were having a very hectic year! All of our girls were in their 20s with children too. I added our Sinead to my school run, taking her to the nursery in Abersychan after taking Daniel to his school. When I went to fetch her later in the mornings, I would ask the staff had she said anything, but every day the answer was no. In September, Ceri gave birth to a bouncing baby boy who they called Connor. We wanted another boy badly in the family to even the gender balance out a bit.

In 1993 it was my turn to hit the big 50. I was offered what I wanted as I didn't like surprise parties or anything like that. I had always wanted to go up in a hot air balloon. Everyone chipped in for it and I got in touch with Flying Colours, a balloon firm from Bristol and arranged a flight on the 1st of May, my birthday. When it came to the day, it had to be cancelled and re-arranged to the 3rd. We started from a hotel near Usk, flew up over Llandegfedd Reservoir, and landed in the Grange, near Cwmbran. There were 12 of us on board and it was a wonderful experience.

The trip to New Zealand was now firmly on. My friend Maxi Nutt and I went to the Thomas Cook shop in Bristol to organise the trip. I was excited to see the British Lions in 1993. We looked at a lot of tour options, but we wanted to do our own itinerary. In June, five of us started out at 7a.m. on a Saturday for the journey of a lifetime. We went to Heathrow Airport heading to the first part of our trip – a 12-hour flight to Bangkok. We stayed there for three nights before moving onto Sydney, Wellington, Auckland, and finishing with five nights in Honolulu on the return trip home. The trip was unbelievable: seeing the Lions beat New Zealand, meeting wonderful people some of whom are still friends; and so many more memories. It was truly a once in a lifetime experience.

After I came back from New Zealand, Sandra and I went on holidays to Saint Ives. We wanted to stay down near the sea. A friend told me to contact Cornish Riviera Holidays and we got a small cottage right down near the beach. It was fittingly named Tee Total Street. We parked the car up and never got off the beach. There was hot weather all week.

Helen had got a job at a Dental Hospital in Birmingham starting that December. She worked there for three years and after winning a national competition for making a special dental piece she secured a very good position in the Dental Hospital in Leeds in September 1996. I borrowed a van and moved her. She went to live in temporary accommodation with friends in Calverley, near Leeds. She stayed there until Christmas when we moved her into Hyde Terrace Hospital Residence. She made some great friends there. While she lived in Birmingham, we visited her quite often and she also spent time back at home whenever she could.

In early 1994, I took up fly fishing. Not knowing anything about it, I had to seek someone who had the patience to teach me. I contacted Cliff Thomas who had once worked with me on a job. He was a plasterer and took me under his wing. He took me to a new trout lake which had opened in Newport, and I was hooked as the saying goes. After catching my first trout and meeting other local blokes we soon travelled all over the place to fish. I had to keep a book to keep track of people who wanted fish. Our grandchildren were the highlight of our lives our Daniel was now 8, Sinead 5, Chloe 3, and Connor 2.

One Sunday in March 1994 at the Royal Oak – the meeting place for all rugby matters, we decided to go to London for the game against England the following week. It was a bit late notice, but I rang a hotel near Piccadilly and booked ten of us for a single night the following Saturday. The following week we caught the train to London. We only had one ticket for the match between us and had a draw which I won! I went to the game on my own. Wales lost but won the championship. I came back to the group after the match and found most of the others drunk out of their minds. Someone suggested we go to the East End which we did, but it was quite intimidating. So, we quickly headed back to Soho to see the goings on there instead. While there I met some boys who I knew from rugby and while talking to them a police car came up slowly looking at us. In my mad ways I flashed the V sign to them and the next thing I knew I was in the back of the car and being locked up for the night. At first, I was in a cell on my own but as the night progressed it filled up with all the idiots in London. I soon realised when they arrested me that they hadn't emptied my pockets, so I still had my wallet and all my money on me. I wanted to shut my eyes, but I was afraid. Sometime later they took me out and I was read the riot act. They let me out and when I asked which way Piccadilly was, I was told to find it myself. When I eventually got there, I was very hungry and there was only a Burger King open, so I went in. It was full of drunk men and ladies of the night. I was afraid to get my wallet out again, so I just quickly got a bag of chips and left.

In 1995 our rugby coach at the time, Alan Archie Evans, a former Welsh player said he'd heard from a team in the United States that were looking to play a game in Wales as part of a rugby tour in the spring. They were a team I had previously coached called Doylestown RFC. We jumped at the idea as it could give us the opportunity of returning this fixture in the future in the USA. We were to have their players stay with us. The team arrived the same weekend as Wales played England in Cardiff. We met the players in our club, and I housed two of them, Jim Meyers a U.S. Marine and Zach an older guy and a committee man. They were perfect gents. We played on the Friday after they arrived which was a very wet and muddy day. I fetched Jim home to change, and we went out for the night. Unknown to Jim, Sandra washed his dirty rugby kit and when he saw the clean kit waiting for him the following day, he just couldn't believe the hospitality. We had a great time and good relations were formed between the teams. We took them to Cardiff on the Saturday just to experience the international atmosphere before they left on the Sunday. It was a good weekend.

For holidays in 1995 we decided to go to Italy. We went to a beautiful resort in Sorrento. While having a drink in the afternoon we chatted to a couple who had been on our flight. They were June and Bernard Howells. What started out as a small chat would soon turn into years long friendship. They were on our table for evening meals, and we ended up going to many places together. We had a wonderful holiday. On arriving home, Sandra sensed there was something wrong with Lynne and Chrissy when Chrissy picked us up from the airport alone. We learned soon after that sadly their marriage was over.

The next year's holiday (1996), Sandra and I went to Brixham. We first stopped off in a flat overlooking the harbour. We travelled around the local area, and I went fishing on a boat. I met TV celebrities Chas & Dave. I didn't recognise them at first and thought they were just regular blokes when they told me they had worked in Usk. I just thought they were building workers and very nice guys. When I got off the boat Sandra took a photo of me with them, and then everybody around wanted one too.

In April 1997 our Ceri gave birth to a beautiful baby girl who she called Cerys. We went on holidays to Benidorm, staying in a self-catering hotel. It was in February and the weather was great. We went to a lot of night spots and bars. Uncharacteristically for her, Sandra got drunk one night and was singing all the way back to our hotel. Later in the year we went up to Yorkshire and stayed in a lovely cottage in Haworth. Helen stayed with us, and we had a wonderful week with her. Our Christmases were the same every year with Helen coming home and all up our Lynne's house in the night.

On the 15th of March 1997, I took Paul Hobbs fishing with me on Saturday morning. On the way home, I stopped to get some chips before rushing home to watch Wales play England in the Royal Oak. By the time I arrived at the pub, the crowd had had a lot of drink. I stayed for the rest of the evening and was late getting home (about 1 o'clock in the morning). That night, I had terrible chest pains and a tingling in my arms, so I went downstairs and shouted for Sandra. She came quickly and could see I was in trouble. She called 999 for help. While she was waiting on the door, a police car stopped, and an officer came in. They gave me a bag to breathe in. The ambulance came and took me to the Royal Gwent Hospital. I had had a heart attack. They gave me some clot busting drugs and I was in intensive care for three days, then coronary care for a week, before they let me home the following Saturday. The rugby boys came to take the mick out of me and to wish me a speedy recovery. A lucky, near miss.

In August '97, we went to the Sicily Isles again. This time we had booked a self-catering place on Buzza Street, and we were going over there by helicopter. We caught the train from Newport to Penzance because after my heart attack it was decided it was too far for me to drive. We stayed the night in the same B&B we had on our previously trip before getting a taxi to the heliport the next day.

In 1998, all the fundraising by the club and especially by Gary Cleverly was all underway for our tour to the USA. In May '98 we had managed to raise something in the region of £7,000 for all players and committee members to go for free. We were flying to Newark, NJ, and stayed at a Days Inn. On the tour, we played against Doylestown RFC who we had hosted in '95, then Blackthorn RFC before heading into New York to finish off. It was a very successful tour. There wasn't a missed word, just a laugh a minute all the way through. One unlucky incident on the tour was when Nick Powell got knocked down by a car on our first night there. He was taken to a trauma unit in Philadelphia where we were staying. He made a quick recovery and returned to us after a few days before flying home.

While we were there, one of the boys who played golf decided to try and book a day's golf for a few of us. He managed to book a golf course some distance away that could accommodate 16 of us and supplied golf clubs for hire. We ordered a couple of taxis and off we went. The taxis left immediately after we got to our destination. Our leader, who had organised the day went to reception, but they told us they weren't open to visitors and knew nothing of our booking. We were in the wrong place. That said, the place was very hospitable, and they went out of their way to get us some member's clubs and let us play a round. Our last destination on the tour was New York. We had a fabulous tour of the amazing city and had the experience of going up to the top of the twin towers.

In late November, our Helen was living in Leeds and hadn't been very well. Sandra was quite worried and had a feeling something was very wrong. On a Friday morning, Sandra phoned Helen who seemed very ill. Immediately, Sandra said she'd have to go to Leeds to see her. I took her to Cwmbran Station and off she went. Helen lived in a nurse's home called Hyde Terrace, not far from Leeds General Infirmary, where she worked. When Sandra got to her flat, her friends, who were nurses, had called an ambulance to take her to hospital. After some hours in A&E and some x-rays, the consultants diagnosed Helen with kidney problems. It turns out she had contracted some form of E. coli. However, the symptoms Helen was showing were problems that weren't usually associated with someone young and fit. The consultants couldn't find where the problems were coming from. Helen had a number of weeks on dialysis and although I visited, it was Sandra more than I who stayed with Helen. She was pretty much staying in Helen's flat for the time Helen was in hospital.

On Christmas Eve, Sandra came back to Wales, and then we both went back to Leeds on Christmas afternoon to take Helen out of hospital. Helen's boss, Dave Langley and his wife Jane let us all stay in his bungalow. She went back into hospital the following day and on 29th of December Helen came out of hospital. We stayed in a Travelodge that night before coming home to Wales on the 30th, the day of her birthday.

Moving into 1999, Helen recovered well at home until Easter when she received a letter to go back to Leeds to have an operation on her pancreas. She came back home for a short stay after the operation. Despite these setbacks, Helen still managed to pass her degree and come the next November we went to Manchester for her graduation. We also moved her from her place in Leeds into a house she had purchased in Pudsey – that was exactly 12 months to the day that Sandra went to Leeds with the bad news of her ill health. What a year that was for us and her!

In 1999 Wales hosted the Rugby World Cup. We reached the quarter finals where we played Australia and lost 9-24. I went to the game and took our Daniel, my grandson, with a friend of mine and his son. It gave the boys an insight into an international match in Cardiff, and it was an unforgettable experience.

Over the years, our girls always wanted a pet, and a rabbit was always at the top of the agenda. The first rabbit was called Malcolm. I had built a hatch with a Perspex panel for the front. In the cold weather we fetched the hutch in. Although we had called the rabbit Malcolm, everyone thought it was a girl. As it got older, it got very big, and at one time developed a large lump. The girls were worried, so we took it to the vet in Usk. Sandra took it in, and I consoled the girls, as we assumed it would have to be put down. When Sandra reappeared with the rabbit, she had a big smile on her face. She told the vet of a big growth on the rabbit only to be told the rabbit was a buck. The big limp was that rabbit's testicles! From that point, it was called

Buck Jones. Later he died of old age, and we got another one called Lady who we had no trouble with. The last rabbit we had was a cheeky thing that growled at anyone who went near him. He followed me everywhere around the garden. After he passed too, the rabbits seemed to just be all mine, so we gave them up. RIP.

In the year 2000, after much deliberation, we as a club, Pontyfelin RFC decided to merge with another local club, Panteg RFC. At the time a lot of our older players were thinking about retiring from the game. It was getting difficult to replace them and the level of rugby we were playing at was slowly diminishing. There were a lack of boys taking up the game, so we took our great knowledge of organising events with us and as we had been doing for the previous number of years, we finished the season with our own seven-a-side tournament which was known throughout the area as the Pontyfelin Sevens. It was an event which we ran for many years, and made us well needed funds, all the while being a great day out for everyone. When we joined Panteg, it seemed they let us run the rugby side of the club and Panteg ran the clubhouse activities.

In 2000 we also went on holiday to Benidorm for the second time and stayed in a hotel. There was plenty to do and the weather was also very good. We also went up to Helen's new house in Pudsey and visited Whitney Bay for a day out. The new millennium felt like a strange thing with people guessing computers were going to break and go wrong, but the year passed by, and all was well.

In February of 2001 Hand, Foot and Mouth disease was discovered in some parts of the country and spread quickly across the UK. It turned out to be disastrous for the farming community. Daniel was getting very good in his rugby career and was playing for Talywain before going onto Pontypool Colts. He was also getting noticed at district level. Daniel had been living with Sandra and I for over a year and we didn't mind at all. He felt like the son I'd never had. Daniel had moved in in 1999 when he was 13 going on 14. He came down to stay for a few days with us and liked it so much that he decided to stay until he was 26! I was still going fishing with my friends: Bernard Price, the Lord Carl Ilsle; and Brian Gregory. Those were good times.

In 2001, I had a lot of unstable anginas and the doctor thought I should have an angiogram. I had a letter to report to Cardiology in the University Hospital Wales where I was to have the procedure. I had the angiogram and there seemed to be a blocked artery, for which I would have to have a stent fitted. They said they'd like to do the procedure there and then as I was there. The stent would open the artery and help my angina problem. They went ahead and did the job. I had to stay in for the night and they informed Sandra immediately. I came home the following day after a visit to the cardiology department for a check-up. The following week I was confronted by a senior nurse called Leslie Davis who asked me if I would be interested in doing a drug trial for heart research under her and doctor W.J. Penny. I said no problem and I started the trial on the 30th of May in 2002. There were follow ups every six months for five years. It was like having an MOT for my body every six months and made life very reassuring. The trial was for a tablet I am now taking which is called Ramipril.

In May 2001, Colin Nash and Rusta Bridges asked me if I would like to join them on a fishing trip to Ireland. The destination, Galway. We'd fish in Lough Corrib, and travel via the ferry in Fishguard. When we got off the ferry, port security pulled us over and enquired if we had any meat or dairy products in our camper. We replied no, but they wanted to search us. There was nothing we could do about it, and Rusta was mad because he had loaded this up with a week's supply of bacon, steak, and burgers; around £60 worth of food in total. They confiscated the lot. Rusta was disgusted and said, "I hope you choke on it!" They only laughed. We got to Galway late in the day and parked up near this big lake.

The following day we found someone who we could hire a boat from, and the day after we took off on this lake. The chap who we hired the boat from said not to go far out because you could get lost. The weather was lovely, and we caught a few fish. The following day we went to Galway to have a look around and a couple of pints of the black stuff. We headed around to the other side of the lake, to a place where they had made the film, The Quiet Man. It was a village called Cong in County Mayo, near Ashford Castle. We went on the lake again but didn't manage to catch any fish. We had a look around Ashford Castle and spent another night in Cong.

The following day, we made a move to meet up with the Talywain Golf boys, who were staying in a place called Tullamore, the county town of County Offaly which is situated in the middle of Ireland. We met up with them and had a drink in a hotel called The Bridge House, a place we'd all come back to in the future.

In July 2001, after visiting Helen in Leeds, I suggested she get a small porch on the front of her house she had in Pudsey. I got to work getting some plastic windows and a door. My friend, Mark Jones (Sparky), took the materials up one Saturday and Daniel and I went up on the Monday to do the job. It was very enjoyable for me to work with my grandson, something a lot of men have never done or get the chance to do. We finished the job and had a day to go fishing. The fishing day didn't start very well when I put the rods on the roof of the car and drove off without thinking. That was the last we saw of those rods. We still managed to go fishing though. As I knew the owner of the lake, he supplied us with some new rods, and we managed to have a great day.

September 2001 saw one of the world's biggest tragedies when two jet aircrafts flew into the two world trade centres, the twin towers. This event killed thousands of people in New York, USA, but the impact was felt across the world. The terrorists also caused untold havoc elsewhere. I was fishing at that particular time with my friend, Bernard Price on Llandegfedd Reservoir. It was the work of world terrorism, a blight on the new world. To think I had been on top of the towers 2 years previous was a scary thought.

In 2002, we had a lot of very big birthdays in our family. We wanted to celebrate Sandra's 60th birthday, so we booked a holiday with a travel company. We had a tour planned out in the United States. We started in California, going from Los Angeles to Las Vegas, where we stayed in the Stratosphere Hotel. We stayed there for five nights before going onto Palm Springs for one night and sightseeing. Then it was onto Santa Barbara for two nights to see the QE2. After this, it was back to Los Angeles, sightseeing all the way before ending the tour in San Francisco for a five-night stay, taking in the Bay Area along the way. The trip was amazing, so much to see and a wonderful holiday.

When we came home from our America trip, our girls had organised Sandra's friends and the family to come for a party on the Sunday of her birthday. She had always wanted a black Labrador dog, and my friend Brian Gregory was a big man with dogs. He had won trials, and his dogs were regarded as some of the best in the area. We had a dog waiting in his kennels who was 12 weeks old. Brian was going to keep him for himself but changed his mind. He said to me he would give Sandra the dog for her birthday. So, on that particular Sunday, he told our Lynne to go home with him from the pub to get the dog for Sandra. Lynne came through our door with the dog, and he went straight up to Sandra. "Whose dog is this?" she said. "Yours!" was the reply. She couldn't believe it! That dog, which we called Frazer, changed our lives for the next 12 years, for all our family, but especially me. He kept me going and must've added years to my life as I took him out every day of the year.

After we had got used to having a dog at home, I spent a lot of time training him to be obedient; a task that was quite easy. As he was a Labrador, he was very clever. Daniel was now playing district rugby for Pontypool District, and I was spending a lot of time taking him to games on a Saturday morning. Life felt hectic as I sometimes struggled to get back down to Panteg afterwards to help out there. After a while, I decided to step down from my commitment with Panteg and concentrate on watching and helping our Daniel.

I got a kennel for the dog down at the bottom of the garden with a wire run on the side. In his sleeping side, I lined it out with insulation to keep him warm. We had a child gate on the back door to keep him in the garden, but as the winter came on, we brought him inside during the day, and put him back down the kennel at night. Come Christmas, Sandra said to bring him inside over the holidays, and that was that. Frazer never went back into his kennel again, and so I sold it. If I hadn't, I think I might have ended up in there myself a few times. Having a dog makes it very difficult to go on holidays, as you have to get someone to look after it. We went to the Sicily Isles again in 2003 and kennelled the dog in Windy Ridge Blaenavon which was a good boarding kennel. Daniel started working part time in Robert Price in Newport and trained with Newport Rugby Academy twice a week.

2003 was my 60th birthday year. I'm not one for parties or surprise occasions, so I said if I was to have something to remember it by, I'd have a personalised number plate for my car. I organised it and I got the plate with my initials H4 GLJ.

That year we went to Ireland again and did so for the next number of years. We went to Ireland when they were against us in the Six Nations in Cardiff. I went with the older players from Talywain Rugby Club, a great bunch of chaps. We held kangaroo courts which I was the judge of and had good fun. The last time I went, was when Wales played Ireland in Croke Park. My days of touring were coming to an end. At the same time Daniel was now playing rugby with Pontypool United Youth, the district side, and he was getting noticed by the Welsh Youth selectors. In February 2004 Daniel received a letter from the Welsh Youth team saying he had been selected to represent them in the European Four Nations tournament. The games would be in Wales and there would be a future tournament in Belfast for the Home Nations Tournament in April. I made good friends with the other boys' fathers who our Daniel played with. The dads would be stood on the touchlines as they trained. With the trip to Belfast coming up, four of us: myself, Mark Wilkes (Wilksy), Chris Lampet (Lampet), and Mike Preece did a group booking and itinerary. Mike booked it all and we followed the boys, flying up to Belfast on Good Friday 2004. We stayed the first night in a B&B near Newtownards, about 10 miles from Belfast. After staying in a B&B for the first night, we were booked into a self-catering farmhouse for the rest of our stay. What a great place it was! We followed the three games the Welsh boys played and won against Scotland, Ireland and best of all, England. We got on well together and being all rugby chaps ourselves, we liked a pint of the black stuff. Other parents of the boys followed us around, and we had some good fun and sing songs. Sadly, it had to finish, but beating England with our Daniel scoring the last try of the game was a massive bonus! After we came home, the Welsh Youth arranged a dinner for all players and families, where we could say our farewells to one and all. I was lucky to see Daniel play with Welsh Youth, as that was the last year they played. Welsh Youth was disbanded and replaced by the Under 20s team.

Around this time, I had gotten into a daily routine of walking the dog. He was ready to go at 6:30 to 7a.m. every morning. We would go out for about nearly an hour, and then after lunch we would sometimes go again depending on the weather. Finally, last thing at night we'd go for a short run, so no-one can say Frazer wasn't well exercised. As Brian Gregory said, it will put ten years on your life, and it certainly has.

After playing for the Welsh Youth in 2004, Daniel continued working for Robert Price part-time, while also playing for Newport Gwent Dragons

Academy part-time. After a while his contract was finished with the Academy, and that left him looking for a full-time job. He didn't know what he wanted to do, so I gave a few guys in the building industry I knew a call. I remember saying to Ade Waters, "Give him a chance, if he's no good after a month get rid of him." So, he started with Adrian Waters. Luck had it that he started with a guy called Richie Jones who took him under his wing, this was while he was working at the Royal Gwent Hospital. Our Daniel was set. They got on well and what he learned off Richie has made him what he is today.

In 2005 we were visiting Helen in Leeds and while looking around B&Q I started looking at kitchens. From that visit our Helen ended up with a new kitchen in the sale. This meant a few days in Pudsey when the materials were delivered. I went up to Leeds on a Monday to fit the kitchen. I did all the plumbing myself. This was something I could do well, and it feels nice to be able to help your children out.

That summer I was invited to go to Ireland with the Rusta Bridges, Tom, who was a scrap merchant; and his cousin Tom, who was a lay preacher. We were heading for a small town called Ballinrobe also in the county of Mayo, like our last visit. We were to fish Lough Mask, a large lake; and we did a bit of touring about. I was asked to go because Rusta couldn't drive, and Tom, the scrap merchant, couldn't read the signs. So, it was left to Tom the preacher and I to share the driving. It was a very long drive after the ferry, but a beautiful place. Rusta had booked a large self-catering house which had its own grounds and was just a couple of miles from the town. It didn't take us long to get on with the locals with Rusta's skills of getting on with everyone and me not far behind. We fished the lough for a few days but didn't have any luck. We went to Cong, the town Rusta and I had been to previously. We again went on the trail of The Quiet Man film. We enjoyed the stay in Ireland. When Rusta and I wanted a drink, Tom, the preacher would drive to a pub and the landlord would open up just for us (even in the mornings), so that Rusta and I could watch the British Lions play. The drive was a long way back to where we were staying, but in Tom's big Mercedes, I was very comfortable.

In 2006, after travelling all around the world and sightseeing, our Helen decided to settle down and look for a partner. She found one in a chap called Nick Beavers, a very nice chap who worked as a chef. He was from Huddersfield. We continued to go up to see her in Pudsey and she came down as often as she could. After playing a few games for Pontypool RFC, our Daniel started playing for Pontypool United to get more experience in the game. We went to the Scilly Isles for holidays again as we'd fallen in love with the islands. I had all one would want in life. I enjoyed going out with Alec Hicks wreck fishing.

In 2007, I received a telephone call from a company called Synexus and was asked if I had high cholesterol. I explained that I took a high dose of atorvastatin for it. They asked if I could go and have some tests, and if I was interested in trialling some new drugs to help reduce high cholesterol. I went to see if I was suitable for the programme. I ticked all the boxes and started on an 18-month trial. It was an injection trial. I had to inject myself in the stomach once every two weeks and fill in a programme chart. I didn't mind as they paid me for every visit I had to make to the centre. This had to be done every 12 weeks for a complete check-up. The results came back after about two years, and they were pleased to say the trial was a huge success.

Later in the year, as I was going up Freehold Land Road, I saw a terraced house with a for sale sign on it. I let our Daniel know and we went to have a look at it. An old lady, Mrs Gibbs had lived in the house, so we contacted the family and they said we could put in an offer for the house. The offer was £65,000. Daniel had a lot of problems getting a mortgage from the banks and his mom helped him with the deposit. Things were very slow going. It was May until we could get in there to start work. I had the bit between my teeth to get going. Richie Jones who Daniel worked with, and I managed the work and got building regulations; a must when doing remedial works. It took a few years, and the work was done by Daniel's father Chrissy and his friends Nicky Jones and Mike Brooke along with a few sub-contractors, also not for getting Tony Cook.

In my many walks with my dog Frazer, I got very friendly with another dog man, Fred Wildgust who lived down in Churchwood. He was a very interesting man from the north of England and while putting the world to right together one day we discussed the pollution of the Avon Lloyd River. It was particularly bad near the corner of Hospital Road. We thought the river was being contaminated from a nearby sewage tank controlled by Welsh Water. Fred contacted Lynne Neagle, our A.M. for Welsh Water who agreed that work would need to be carried out and they upgraded the storm tanks and sorted the problem out.

2008 was going to be a happy year of two weddings, but in March of that year Darrel, our Lynne's partner's mum was struck suddenly by a tragedy. She died suddenly on holiday in Scotland, just weeks before the wedding day. They got married in May and it was a sad but a great occasion. The second wedding was to be between Helen and Nic who were getting married later in the year. Nic's parents came down one weekend and we all went out looking for venues for the event. We went to Tintern Abbey Hotel, which later went bankrupt, the Manor Hotel in Crickhowell, and GreenMeadow Golf Club in Cwmbran. After much deliberation, and our Lynne's advice, the Parkway Hotel was chosen. The date was set for October and the whole day went off fine. Friends came from all over the country for a wonderful day.

We continued working on our Daniel's house. Our Connor came across to give me a hand one day. I showed him what I was doing and then had to go off the job. When I came back, he had finished what I was doing. I quickly marked him down as having good potential.

In the spring of 2009, after having problems putting our dog in kennels while we went on holidays, we decided to get a caravan. We got a cheap thing to start with, but it turned out not to be worth it. So, we got another one, an old Mayfly. Not being used to caravanning, there was a steep learning curve, but it was also good fun. Our first trip was to Warren farm, near Weston. I soon got the hang of towing and along with the dog, off we went. It proved a good plan and we settled into a different way of holidaying. The dog was good and there was plenty of space to walk him. Over the next few years, we went to Pandy, West Wales, and Devon, and really enjoyed every trip. The dog was now getting too old to go in the van, so we went for a few years staying in holiday cottages in West Wales up to the time he passed away in 2014.

2009 was also the year I started having a lot of trouble with pain in my back, hip and groin. I asked Doctor Machado, my doctor, if I could take some ibuprofen painkillers. He examined me, asked a few questions, and said he would refer me to Mr Greg Jones, an orthopaedic surgeon. It would be a bit of a wait, but I went to see him come September. After some x-rays, he said my hips were in a bad condition, and he would let me know when he could do surgery.

While out walking with Frazer one morning I came home and fell ill. I sat down in the chair and passed out. Sandra sent for our Lynne and Daniel. They sent for an ambulance who took me to the Royal Gwent. I was in for two days before being sent home. The doctor I saw read a report that said I had had a fit. "Rubbish!" was his reply. He arranged for me to have some more scans at Saint Woolos Hospital, and a cat scan at Royal Gwent. The results came back, and they showed that I had had a slight stroke that morning, and I had previously had a bleed that I didn't know about. After visiting

Saint Woolos hospital a few times, I was thankfully given the all-clear. The dog was still keeping me fit and we were going for daily walks. Helen became pregnant in and was expecting in November. Sandra went up as usual in the summer, and then went up on the 28th of November for the delivery. Helen gave birth that day to a beautiful boy, Euan Beavers, a day before his dad's birthday.

I received a letter in January 2010 to go to Saint Woolos Hospital to have a preliminary examination for the hip replacement ordered by Greg Jones. I was becoming quite a regular at the Hospital. They explained that the procedure would have to be done at the Royal Gwent because of my heart condition. They told me they would contact me in the near future. I then received a letter to report to the DT East Ward at the Royal Gwent for admittance on a Friday. The procedure wasn't planned until the Monday, but I was needed for the weekend so they could monitor me. On the Monday of my op, I saw Greg Jones. His sidekick painted my left hip and told the nurse to get me ready for the afternoon. I was gowned up and the afternoon came around, but there was no sign of anyone even close to 4 o'clock. A male nurse appeared and said, "Do you want the good news or the bad?" Something had gone wrong in the theatre, and I could go home. It was all off. I was not an amused bunny at all. I had to wait another eight weeks before going through the same process again.

The next time I went down the epidural didn't sedate me properly, and I felt quite ill for a few days after the operation. It didn't go well at all, and I had to stay in for over a week because of an infection. That said, after I came out, I was on my feet in no time at all. I was glad to get out and once again taking Frazer for daily walks helped massively with getting me back to full fitness. I continued to work up our Daniel's house and we now had permission from a structural engineer to go ahead with a loft conversion. We did this to make another bedroom. The bathroom had been refurbished and a new roof put on. Thankfully we were still getting a lot of help from friends with the project.

I had to go back to see Greg Jones again in 2011 for another hip replacement (my right one this time). He said it could be done in six months. I waited until I received a letter in October from Mr Jones telling me he couldn't do my second hip replacement. He suggested I contact a new orthopaedic consultant Mr Gordon Gillespie. I did this and his secretary made me an appointment to see him two weeks later. Mr Gillespie was a very nice chap who said he could do my hip in the beginning of December; that was brilliant! What a quick turnaround compared to last time! I went to the Royal Gwent on the 10th of December and had it done no problem. I was out within a week, but this time it took a while again to get back on my feet. Pretty soon I was out walking the dog again though.

Our Sinead was now living in Pontycymer with her partner, Rhys, who was a fireman. It was good to see the grandchildren settling down. Chrissy, our Daniel's dad was working hard with his mate Mike on weekends on Daniel's house. We planned a kitchen extension but had to get a build over sewer agreement from Welsh Water. That took a little time, but they agreed to it and the extension was built.

2012 came. Sandra's niece, Joann James had been very ill for some time with cancer. She sadly died from her illness in September. Sandra was in Leeds at the time and came home with Helen, a very sad occasion. Chloe met her future partner, Dav, a chap from Bristol. He was born in Italy, but had spent most of his life in this country, a very nice chap. He was very interested setting up his own business. We once again went to West Wales, this time staying in coastal cottages as we had gotten rid of the caravan. It was a lot easier than the caravan. Our Sinead was pregnant and gave birth to a beautiful baby girl in October; Ava May, who was our first great-grandchild.

Also in 2012, Daniel and his partner Leanne finally moved into his house on Freehold Land Road. There was still a lot of external work to do on the house, but after living with us for 12 years it was odd to see him leave. Daniel was a regular in the Pontypool RFC team as a professional player. That year Pontypool was relegated to the newly formed First Division, after it was deemed their record over the last six seasons wasn't good enough. In the following season 2012-13 Daniel went to play for Newport in the Welsh Premier Division. He played for Newport for three seasons before returning to Pontypool.

For some time in 2013 I had been having a lot of chest infections which had led to a few overnight stays in hospital. The x-ray showed I had COPD, a complaint derived from smoking even though I had stopped smoking in 1988. I was given an inhaler in March which helped.

2013 also saw the death of Chrissy, our grandchildren's father. He had been at home with his new wife, Sue when she went into the kitchen and found him collapsed on the floor. He had had a massive heart attack and died. The paramedics came quickly but said even if they had been on the scene as it happened, they couldn't have saved him. It was a devastating loss to everyone who knew him. He was such a lovely man; gentle and kind. Sandra and I loved him like a son and his children have never gotten over it. To commemorate Chrissy our Daniel, Sinead and Chloe made a bench at Blaenserchan Colliery. It was a place Chrissy loved to go and the bench was a beautiful commemoration to remember him by. It's fitting that everyone who walks up that way always refers to the bench as Chrissy's bench.

Our Helen gave birth to another boy, Thomas Beavers in May. We went to Abercastle, West Wales for our holidays with the dog. Frazer was really slowing down by that point and struggling to jump into the car. Speaking of cars, for the last number of years, Gareth Cleverly had been supplying my cars and religiously kept them on the roads in perfect condition.

As Christmas 2013 approached, I noticed that Frazer was struggling when we were out for a morning walk, and when he ate his food. We now had an iPad, something we didn't really want, but our Lynne's children paid for it. It was a Christmas present for us. We were unsure when we went to Cardiff to get it, and it took some time to sort it out, but now it's the best thing we've ever received.

After a very good Christmas with all the family, our beloved dog Fraser went downhill fast. Sandra and I spoke about what the best thing to do was. We agreed to speak to the vet. We discussed his situation and agreed that when the time came to put him out of pain, we would ring the vet to come to the house and put him to sleep. A week or so later I took him out one morning and he could only walk a few steps before sitting down. I tried to encourage him, but he was struggling big time. When I got home, I said to Sandra, "I think the time has come." He was 12 years old and what 12 years he had given us. We called Daniel and he agreed we should ring the vet who came and did his job. Everyone was gutted it was like losing a member of our family.

In February 2014 we went up to our Helen's because she was having an operation on her hand. We came back after a few days, on a Thursday. On the way back, I fell ill and had to go to bed. I had a bad chest infection again, but after some antibiotics I was feeling a little better. However, it didn't clear it up completely, and I was soon seeing a nurse again who prescribed something stronger, Doxycycline with steroids. That seemed to sort it out.

We had booked a holiday to the Scilly Isles for the end of April, and while we were away a painter was going to decorate our lounge. The day before we were due to go, we packed our cases and cleared the lounge. We moved all the furniture ready to go that night, but then I was suddenly taken ill again! I had a job to breathe and a very high temperature. With the situation I was in, there was no way I was going anywhere. So, Sandra took control and put all the furniture back in place. She rang the doctor's when they opened and had to cancel all the holiday bookings. The doctor came and said that the chest sample I had given them that week showed double pneumonia.

It was a bit of luck that we hadn't gone away as the double pneumonia took a long time to get over. One consolation was that for Helen's Thomas' first birthday all the family went up to Leeds as a surprise visit to celebrate it. Plans were being made for our Sinead's wedding near Christmas. It was going to be in the little church in Coed-y-Paen on the 23rd of December 2014 with the reception after in the nearby pub, The Carpenter's Arms. It was an unbelievable day out after a very trying year.

Into 2015 and Leanne, Daniel's partner gave birth to our first great-grandson, Jack Robinson in April. The family kept growing every year. I was now having problems with my right hip. I saw the consultant of my first hip replacement who gave me an x-ray. They found a fragment of bone on my hip which would have to be removed. So, it was off to the Royal Gwent again. We also went on holiday to Brean in Somerset in our Lynne's caravan.

In 2016 our two granddaughters were pregnant. First, our Chloe had a baby boy in May. Her and her partner Dav were ecstatic! He was a beautiful boy named Ziah, very Italian! In July, our Sinead gave birth to an equally beautiful boy, Noah. We now had four great-grandchildren and our family kept getting bigger and bigger. Cerys and her partner were getting on fine with Lloyd doing very well in the Royal Navy. He also looked very likely to be going to the top with all the exams he had passed too!

I was offered one of the small, raised plots of green up at the local allotments in 2016. It was built from lottery grants and was for disabled people. There was a greenhouse and a shed for use too which was an excellent help for older people. There was always someone to help you or offer advice, and I grew a lot of veg, such as onions and beetroot. I also started making walking sticks as a hobby and was fortunate enough to sell a few. I did a few boot sales and enjoyed the banter of trying to make a pound or two. I still had my greenhouse and runner beans in my back garden. Sandra was now over the moon to have another great-grandson to spoil and take for walks.

This was also the year Welsh football did well in the European Cup, even beating England. This was the main joy of our Connor who followed Wales and was part of the Welsh Barmy Army. In August we went on holiday to the Edinburgh Military Tattoo Festival. We went via coach tour and had a wonderful time. It was Daniel's 30th birthday in November and as a surprise visit, we went to Bluestone Theme Park to celebrate. Sadly, in November after a short illness Sandra's sister, Barbara Panzer died in her 90s.

For 2017's holiday, we booked another trip to the Sicily Isles. After having to cancel the 2014 trip because of my illness, I was hoping this trip would be more successful. This time we were travelling to Exeter and then catching a small plane to the Sicily Isles. Sandra at this time was suffering from what turned out to be polymyalgia, a very painful condition only treated with steroids over a long period of time. I must mention my doctor, Doctor Machado from Abersychan Group Practice in the diagnosis of Sandra's illness. He really looked after her, a thing he has also done for me. I trust him in every way, and he has kept me alive without a doubt.

Our Helen in Leeds had been looking for a bigger house to move to. She wanted to stay in the same area, Pudsey where the boys were settled in school, and where her husband, Nic was also teaching. They found a nice house not far from where she had lived some years before. The day of the move our grandchildren went up in force to help. Connor and Daniel, both carpenters, did some work in the new house and the result was the move went like clockwork thanks to some good organisation.

One morning in August 2017 I didn't feel very well after having my breakfast, so I went outside to get some fresh air in the garden. I had very bad chest pain, so I came back in, and Sandra got me to sit down. She rang the emergency services and in no time a paramedic appeared and took over. He gave me some aspirin and the next thing I remember I was in the back of an ambulance on Oxygen. They were arranging for me to go into hospital and were already waiting for me at the Royal Gwent. They discovered my heart was in arrhythmia and they were planning on stopping and restarting it, but luckily my heart went back to normal. I was sent for an angiogram after this, and they found I had four blockages in my arteries. I would have to have a bypass. I was then sent to the intensive care unit and after a while the heart consultant told me I was going to the University Hospital of Wales. Sandra came with me, and I was admitted in the afternoon. I was in the ICU for two days before being sent to a ward to wait for the bypass operation.

I felt better there and caused them some problems with the music on my iPad. The other patients wanted some country and western music. After a few warnings and some yellow cards, I was transferred to a single room to keep me quiet. My consultant Miss Deglurkar told me I would have to have a quadruple bypass and an ICD unit fitted in my left shoulder to prevent future arrhythmia. I had my bypass op and for 2-3 days I didn't know where I was. I had a lot of nightmares and hallucinations. I was somewhere other than in hospital. After four weeks in, I was sent home to get back to health. After some good looking after, it wasn't long before I was back to my old self. I went to the heart rehab in County Hospital and enjoyed that because it gave me back a lot of confidence.

In the early part of 2018, everyone was planning our Lynne's 50th birthday. It was going to be a big event in Cwrt Bleddyn Hotel in Usk. Everyone was in on the planning. It was going to be a masked ball and her children had organised a special floor for dancing on with infill lights. The place would be full of decorations and a lot of guests were staying there. On the night it went off perfectly and everyone enjoyed the occasion.

Sandra and I went to Rhyl and North Wales on a coach trip for a few days. The trip was not very good, apart from going to see Portmeirion, Clough Williams-Ellis' village which was somewhere I always wanted to visit. The trip was far too long, getting there was a hassle. We had to pick people up all over the West Country enroute. It took so long that we decided not to come home on the coach, preferring to catch a train back instead.

In June, we were invited to David Cleverly's wedding night in West Wales. We were very close to David and Bex and it was a great night with Sandra drinking with Ann and company. It was all very unsensible, but we stayed in a B&B.

In September we went for a weekend to London with a coach from Newport. We stayed in the Tower Guoman Hotel and visited the Tower of London, somewhere I had never been to, and the London Eye. From Victoria Coach Station we got a taxi to the hotel and then visited the tower in the early evening. We went for a meal at Tower Bridge Wetherspoons, after which we decided to walk back towards Tower Bridge. When we were near to it, Sandra, who had her arm through mine, fell forward onto her right shoulder. A few people helped her to her feet. I could see she was shaken up, but she wouldn't have any attention. A fire engine that was passing at the time stopped in the central reservation and a fireman ran over to ask if she was alright. Sandra being Sandra refused all the offers of help. So, after a while, we went on our way. We went for a walk around the hotel, and all seemed fine, but the following morning she was in severe pain. I rang the coach company to get an earlier coach home. After a long trip home, she was glad to get into her own house. After seeing our doctor, she saw the consultant, Mr Kulkarny. She had to have shoulder surgery. In November, our Chloe gave birth to another great-grandson, what a cracker, named Zander. The family is growing by the year.

For Christmas of 2019, our Lynne's children invited us to go with them on a holiday in April to North Wales. Some of the party were going to climb Snowden, and we would all be staying in a holiday lodge together. Come April, we set off in four cars and got there in the afternoon. What a beautiful place it was. There was plenty of room for all. We went on a Monday. Tuesday morning Daniel and I went fishing. In the afternoon we all went to Caernarfon to see the castle and have a look around. On Wednesday Daniel, Dav and Sinead got ready to climb Snowden while the rest of us went to Portmerion. Later we went to Llanberis to catch the Snowden Mountain Railway Train to meet the ones who had climbed it on their way back down. We met up with them near the top and had a wonderful photo of the whole group. The three that went up Snowden also went on the North Wales zip wire one afternoon. We came back home on the Thursday, after having a great few days.

It was our Jack's birthday on the 22nd of April. On the day they celebrated his birthday, I was potting some plants in the garden and tripped over a compost bag, injuring my ribs and wrist. I went to the A&E at Neville Hall Hospital and when I finally saw someone after a very long wait, I was told there was nothing they could do for a bruised rib, and I would have to wait to see a doctor. After another long wait I grew annoyed of waiting and couldn't wait any longer. I was picked up from the hospital, came home and went to bed. As the day went on, I developed a chest infection. I'm lucky I carry a rescue pack of antibiotics and steroids to combat these infections. The following morning, my doctor, Doctor Machado came and took a chest sample to be analysed. I soon recovered and in July I had an appointment with a chest consultant who was concerned about my chest problems. He changed the inhaler I was taking, and I was alright for a while, but in the October, I went to the doctor with a rattling chest. He said it was mucus and I had to be put on more antibiotics. After a few weeks, I was back with the same problem. Then in November I saw a chest and heart consultant, Helen Folds. She explained that the chest problems were caused by the mucus and said I would have to take steroids for the rest of my life.

It got worse over the next few weeks, and I had difficulty breathing. I saw something in the paper about some breathing device that could help me, and I got one. It helped me immediately. After this, I was determined to get professional help, and got an appointment with Mr Patrick Flood Page, a chest consultant in Saint Joseph's Hospital in Newport Private. He went through everything with me and said they had taken the wrong inhaler off me. In July I needed a steroid inhaler. He also said my condition was Bronchiectasis and COPD. He also suggested some alteration in my tablets. I had a scan in the following January of 2020 which confirmed all he had told me. Now, I am a lot better all thanks to that visit to Mr Flood Page.

2019's Christmas, our Lynne's family organised a Christmas dinner at the Court Bleddyn Hotel near Usk. It was felt that our family, including our Helen and Lynne's families were too large when altogether to have it in our house. As a result, they booked the Oak Room, somewhere we had been before. We had a wonderful time there and there was a Father Christmas for the children who all received a present. The food and experience were unbelievable and after the meal we booked for 2020 too (but we all now know that that wasn't to happen).

We've hit 2020 and we end where we began. I'm now back to the start of my book in March 2020. There was an initial shock of being told we had to lockdown. First it was for a few weeks, and then some months. There has been a devastating effect as a result of the virus throughout the whole world. The lockdown since March has caused havoc in the supermarkets with a worldwide shortage of toilet paper and other supplies. For some unknown reason, people have been hoarding items. There were huge shortages on most things. We were lucky that we had been having our shopping delivered from Tesco for some years, and the Welsh Government gave people who were shielding priority slots for orders. The only good thing about it all was we were having good weather, so I spent some time in the garden. Family would come and sit outside, and our Conservatory was brilliant as Sandra and I could stay in. The Welsh government lifted the lockdown in August, on the 16th. We had previously booked a few days in West Wales at a B&B, so that gave us a nice break. We also booked a night in a very posh hotel near Crickhowell, Gliffaes Hotel. I fished in the river with a ghillie. Come September, things started to look bleak once again, and it wasn't long before the infection rates started to rise once more. Another lockdown was imminent and that came for a few weeks in November. Christmas was on the horizon, but that didn't happen at all with all the country and hospitals looking like they would never recover.

The place I finish this book is in March 2021. I've had my first vaccine, and as of the day I'm writing this I am to receive the second one. The vaccine has been a world saving moment and perhaps a path that will let us look forward to a better future.

www.ingramcontent.com/pod-product-compliance
Lightning Source LLC
Chambersburg PA
CBHW081459070526
44586CB00019B/2425